ADELPHI
Paper • 307

D1593038

Rethinking Confidence-Building Measures

Contents

Oxford University Press, Great Clarendon Street, Oxford OX2 6DP
Oxford New York
Athens Auckland Bangkok Bombay
Calcutta Cape Town Dar es Salaam Delhi
Florence Hong Kong Istanbul Karachi
Kuala Lumpur Madras Madrid Melbourne
Mexico City Nairobi Paris Singapore
Taipei Tokyo Toronto
and associated companies in
Berlin Ibadan

Oxford is a trade mark of Oxford University Press

Published in the United States
by Oxford University Press Inc., New York

© The International Institute for Strategic Studies 1996

First published December 1996 by Oxford University Press for
The International Institute for Strategic Studies
23 Tavistock Street, London WC2E 7NQ

Director: Dr John Chipman
Deputy Director: Rose Gottemoeller

British Library Cataloguing in Publication Data

Data available

Library of Congress Cataloguing in Publication Data

ISBN 0-19-829321-6
ISSN 0567-932X

GLOSSARY

APEC	Asia-Pacific Economic Cooperation
ARF	ASEAN Regional Forum
ASEAN	Association of South-East Asian Nations
CBMs	Confidence-building Measures
CFE	Conventional Armed Forces in Europe
CSBMs	Confidence- and Security-building Measures
CSCE	Conference on Security and Cooperation in Europe (now OSCE)
CSCM	Conference on Security and Cooperation in the Mediterranean
DGMO	Directors General of Military Operations
INCSEA	Incidents at Sea
MBFR	Mutual and Balanced Force Reduction
NNA	Neutral and Non-aligned Nations
NWFZ	Nuclear Weapon Free Zone
OAS	Organisation of American States
OSCE	Organisation for Security and Cooperation in Europe
RSS	Regional Security System (East Caribbean nations)
SAR	Search and Rescue
WTO	Warsaw Treaty Organisation

INTRODUCTION

Confidence-building measures (CBMs) are often described as the fastest growing business of the post-Cold War era.[1] They are said to be useful instruments for preventing wars, bringing about arms-control and disarmament agreements and facilitating conflict resolution. It is also suggested that they are applicable to all states, easily negotiable and bring only benefits. Given such hyperbolic praise, it is no surprise that CBMs have rapidly become a feature of discussions about international security. Although the term itself only entered the diplomatic language in the mid-1970s, today almost every region of the world is considering or implementing some form of CBM. Judging by how the subject is filling the agenda of diplomatic negotiations, current efforts to implement CBMs are surpassing those made during the Cold War to achieve arms-control agreements.

But are CBMs even half as good as advertised? They do not entail limiting or reducing any numbers of weapons, nor do they suggest disarming any nation. Proponents note that CBMs are only intended as steps towards these goals. They also argue that these measures prevent accidental wars and, by improving trust between rival states or potential adversaries, clear the path to better political and military relations. Clearly CBMs are not intended to deal with the root causes of conflicts, but advocates argue that these measures are the first step in turning hostile relationships into more accommodating ones. It is often said that 'if CBMs won't work, nothing else will'.

Originally, the goals for confidence-building measures were less ambitious – they were intended to address specific military concerns, such as surprise attack. In the European Cold War environment, where the measures were first successfully negotiated, few argued that they would improve trust between adversaries. The Western states who suggested negotiating CBMs in the Conference on Security and Cooperation in Europe (CSCE) (now Organisation for Security and Cooperation in Europe [OSCE]) did not trust their Eastern counterparts in the Warsaw Pact, and they certainly never considered using the tools and techniques of CBMs to bridge the East–West divide.

Things have changed considerably since the end of the Cold War. The same measures – albeit slightly transformed to fit other regional applications – are now looked upon as a useful way of addressing numerous aspects of inter-state relations. CBMs, it is argued, can reduce the risk of miscalculation or communication failure escalating into war, and can inhibit the use, or the threat of use, of force for political coercion. They can increase predictability, strengthen stability and enhance security, as well as open 'channels of communication' between adversaries, break deadlocked security relationships, improve political climates and help establish working relationships. CBMs can also be the basis for establishing cooperative security regimes or collective security systems, for defining new models of security relationships, or for 'reorganising' security. Of course, proponents would not claim that this long (and still only partial) list of benefits applies to all states, at all times or in all situations, but it does highlight the many expectations the concept and its application create.

As this paper will demonstrate, these grandiose expectations are misplaced. Only a handful of existing CBMs even begin to constrain the behaviour of states and make a real contribution to international security. What is worse, the process of negotiating, and sometimes even executing, these measures can actually damage international security. It is not that all CBMs are without value, but rather that they need to be as specific and verifiable as possible.

CBMs are much more complex than is usually recognised. They are not cost-free and do not only bring positive results. This paper argues that in nearly all cases, CBMs are only as strong as the fundamental political will for compromise in any successful negotiations. Without pre-existing *détente*, CBMs are of little value. They cannot create *détente* and under certain circumstances, they can be '*détente-consuming*'. Given the limited diplomatic resources of most states, it may be more useful to focus on arms control. Although the objectives may be more difficult to achieve, the agreements are likely to be more useful in building international security.

The reasons for the exaggerated hopes and ensuing complications surrounding CBMs begin with the very vagueness of the concept. There is no recognised or accepted theory of CBMs, nor have the methods or tools employed changed in any significant way since a few modest measures were agreed at the 1975 CSCE Helsinki Conference. For the purposes of this analysis, CBMs are defined as actions falling into one or more of the following categories:

• exchanging information and/or increasing communication between the parties;
• exchanging observers and/or conducting inspections;
• establishing 'rules of the road' for certain military operations; and
• applying restraints on the operation and readiness of military forces.

From this short list, countless CBMs can be (and have been) devised, but does the multiplication or repetition of any or all of these steps really prevent wars, bring arms control and disarmament, alter long-held patterns of distrust between states and shift relationships from confrontation to cooperation? Are they likely to bring only positive results? In short, is the confidence-building approach an idea whose time has come, or is it a concept overburdened with promises and likely to disappoint?

I. IN SEARCH OF A THEORY: DEVELOPING THE CONCEPT

Unlike other important instruments of foreign and security policy, the 'theory' of confidence-building measures was an afterthought. In contrast to arms control, for instance, which benefited from a conceptual foundation on which to base the practice, the application of confidence-building measures preceded its conceptual exploration. Although there is still no agreed theory of CBMs, it is argued that they can be used in any region by any state, irrespective of the state of their relationships; foes and friends alike, larger or lesser powers, neighbouring countries, members of alliances and participants in regional organisations can all benefit from their implementation.

Origins

To understand why the concept has become so popular, it is necessary to review the different phases of its historical development. The term 'confidence-building measures' entered the diplomatic language following the negotiation of some modest measures during the 1975 CSCE Helsinki Conference. The measures agreed then (often referred to as the 'first generation' of European CBMs) basically related to the exchange of information, notification and observation of major military activities. The 35 participating states, which included all of Europe (except Albania), plus the United States and Canada, agreed to:

- give notice of military manoeuvres exceeding a total of 25,000 troops, 21 days or more in advance;
- invite observers to these military manoeuvres on a voluntary basis; and
- give, voluntarily, prior notification of smaller manoeuvres and major troop movements.[1]

What precisely this 'system' of confidence-building measures was intended to accomplish, however, is uncertain. The Helsinki Final Act ascribed three objectives to the CBMs: to eliminate the causes of tensions; to promote confidence and contribute to stability and security; and to reduce the danger of armed conflict arising from misunderstanding or miscalculation. The incongruence between these lofty objectives and the reality of the Final Act's actual provisions was not simply a reflection of conference rhetoric at a time of *détente*. The former Warsaw Pact nations adamantly opposed any discussion of CBMs in the CSCE, and the Western states, which proposed them, had no clear view of what they wanted to accomplish, or how it was to be done.[2] As its title suggested, the Conference on Security and Cooperation in Europe had to address security issues.[3] But, as several NATO countries objected to the inclusion of anything resembling arms control, the Allies settled on CBMs, the most innocuous of all available alternatives.[4]

This is not to say that there was no potential role for the measures or that the idea was entirely new. As early as 1958, notification of large military manoeuvres and exchange of observers were discussed in the framework of the Conference on the Prevention of Surprise Attack. In the early 1960s, almost identical measures were put forward by both the US and the Soviet Union in an attempt to achieve general and comprehensive disarmament. Finally, a few years before the CBMs were considered for negotiation in the CSCE, similar measures (labelled 'Associated Measures') were studied by the NATO states as part of the Alliance's strategy for its proposed negotiations on the Mutual and Balanced Force Reductions (MBFR) in Europe. What was new about the negotiated CSCE CBMs was just that – they had been successfully negotiated. Indeed, if anything distinguished them from the earlier proposals, it was that the Helsinki measures were to be implemented outside any arms-control framework (and thus independently of any measures related to limiting or reducing forces and armaments), and to be applied voluntarily without any provision for verification.

The Theory After the Practice
Confidence-building measures were introduced by NATO to counter measures sought by the Soviet Union at the 1975 Conference. Western officials were quick to play down the CBMs' military value, suggesting instead that they were political and psychological in nature.[5] With no clear policy statement on their purpose, numerous interpretations of the goals and objectives of CBMs soon emerged. Eventually, in the mid-1970s, a 'theory' took hold in the West. Because military exercises in Europe were conducted in secrecy, they could be mistaken for potentially hostile actions and could trigger confrontation or armed conflict. Observance of 'traffic rules' for routine activities could reduce such risks and 'help separate unambiguous signals of hostile intent from the random noise of continuous military activity'.[6]

This theory implies that the ultimate goal of CBMs was to reduce the risk of surprise attack. The underlying assumption was that a benign activity could be misinterpreted and trigger an undesirable reaction out of fear of a surprise attack – the worst-case scenario from a Western point of view. Also implicit was that information and knowledge about military activities could clarify their true nature, including any underlying intentions. The Final Act recognised that the danger of misinterpretation was particularly significant in a situation where a state lacks 'clear and timely information about the nature of such activities'. Another goal was to inhibit the threat, or use of force, for coercion purposes. CBMs would have the beneficial role of deterring the display of large military forces for political intimidation, or raising the political cost of any Soviet-led intervention in Eastern Europe.

This somewhat idealised concept of what the initial CSCE CBMs could and should accomplish was, of course, tailored by the West. NATO had more to gain from transparency than the Warsaw Pact because of the extreme secrecy in which the Warsaw Treaty Organisation (WTO) operated. Surprise attack was presented as the foremost threat to the Western alliance in its first 40 years of existence, hence its prominence in a developing theory based predominantly on measures devised to make sudden, large military operations more difficult to initiate or to conceal. The Soviet Union had a long history of intervening in the domestic affairs of its 'allies'. Sudden military 'exercises' were a convenient way for the Kremlin to intimidate the Eastern European states and discourage any nascent tendencies to depart from its orbit. Thus, the West thought that by forcing the Soviet Union to announce its 'exercises' in advance, it could constrain Moscow's ability to dominate its neighbours.

Reducing misinterpretation, avoiding the risk of surprise attack, and inhibiting the use of force for political purposes soon became recognised as the three main goals of the European CBMs from which a number of intermediary or related objectives could be derived. Identifying a pattern of military activities would increase predictability and promote stability, which in turn could reduce tensions and mistrust and foster mutual confidence. Several variants were formulated along these lines. Most of these goals, of course, went far beyond what the Western governments had in mind when they proposed the measures. The limited nature of the provisions made meeting any of these objectives almost impossible. Yet, the 1975 Conference concluded with an agreement to hold follow-up review meetings.[7] Thus, not only were CBMs here to stay, but they were to be open to evaluation and possible improvements. Furthermore, they benefited from the attention given to the Conference; this was the only 'military' component of a pact signed by 35 nations which was to gain prominence over the years because of its human-rights provisions.

Arms-Control Impact

Equally important to the development of the CBM concept was the growing disappointment in the late 1970s with the results of arms-control negotiations. In Europe, for instance, the MBFR talks were bogged down for years on what appeared to be an insurmountable East–West dispute relating to the number of troops on each side. If swift agreement on force reduction was too difficult to achieve, less demanding measures to gain knowledge of the level, composition, locations or activities of the military forces appeared to be a viable (if not the only) option for resolving the impasse, or at least laying the foundation for a resolution. The potential contribution of CBMs to improving military 'transparency' (in the East) not only came to be recognised as a much-needed commodity, but also was to receive official backing, which until then had not been particularly forthcoming.[8]

During the same period, as Lawrence Freedman aptly pointed out, CBMs were seized upon 'as the last best hope of arms control' being 'presented as addressing the real issue, fear of surprise attack, rather than the more artificial question of force levels'.[9] Indeed, while the conventional arms-control talks remained deadlocked, they were also increasingly perceived as irrelevant. Powerful political figures, including US Senator Sam Nunn and Congressman Les Aspin, argued at the time that given the rapid pace of military modernisation and the deployment of Soviet military power, reducing troop levels would do little to alleviate the possibility of a surprise attack, while the warning time for such an attack was constantly being reduced.[10] CSCE-type measures implemented *in conjunction* with verification procedures *and* constraints on the use of military forces were then seen as a promising means of addressing these problems.

Finally, given the difficulties of reaching arms-control agreements, shifting attention to restricting military operations, rather than capabilities, opened still more avenues for CBMs. As Christoph Bertram argued in 1978, 'Because it concentrates explicitly on what the other side can do rather than on what military quantities it has at its disposal, this approach represents a fundamental change, a change from a focus on the military input – men, tanks, missiles – to a focus on the military output – surprise attack, pre-emptive nuclear strike, etc'.[11]

From then on, what began as the 'junk food' of arms control[12] was only a step away from becoming 'the other side of the coin'.[13] Presented as 'operational' arms control, CBMs were to complement the 'structural' (or traditional) approach to arms control, dealing primarily with size and composition.[14]

10

Alongside these developments emerged the practice of renaming, or 're-labelling', as CBMs a whole range of military initiatives which were not arms contról *per se* – that is, which did not involve reducing or limiting weapons or forces. This was the case with several US–Soviet bilateral arrangements and proposals, including the 1963 'hot line' agreement establishing a direct communication link between Washington and Moscow, the 1972 Agreement on the Prevention of Incidents at Sea (INCSEA) and the 1955 'Open Skies' proposal by US President Dwight Eisenhower, from which evolved the first use of the term 'confidence-building measures', in a UN resolution that same year.[15]

The purpose of such an exercise remains unclear. Arguably, these initiatives never had, as their new label suggested, the primary objective of 'building confidence' *per se* – a fact which also applied, ironically, to the Helsinki measures. If anything, it was confusing to merge under one label different initiatives or measures previously devised to deal with specific situations or environments. The use of a hot line, for instance, pre-supposes a crisis. This implies very short time restraints where little consideration can be given to 'building confidence', and certainly not in the way the CSCE CBMs were then presumably supposed to do by allowing patterns of military exercises to develop over several years.

The INCSEA agreement also appears to have had little direct relevance to 'confidence-building'. Incidents at sea rarely, if ever, were accidental. They resulted from a military practice of aggressive surveillance and close trailing of each other's forces to gain intelligence or disrupt exercises, which were described by the former US Chief of Naval Operations, Admiral Elmo Zumwalt, as 'an extremely dangerous, but exhilarating, running game of "chicken"'.[16] These operations, furthermore, were often in clear violation of the letter and spirit of International Regulations for Preventing Collisions at Sea ('Rules of the Road'),[17] which by any 'confidence-building' standard – now or then – would be considered one of the most significant measures ever adopted by the international community. Finally, the fact that rival ships would avoid intentionally harassing one another on a regular basis provided little reassurance that they would not be at war in the immediate future; at least, though, they would not be responsible for causing it.

The 'Open Skies' proposal, calling for unrestrained aerial inspection of US–Soviet territory, was developed by the Eisenhower administration as an intelligence measure for gathering accurate targeting data on Soviet strategic nuclear forces. This was to ensure the success of any US nuclear counter-attack, which certainly casts doubts about the true nature of the search for 'mutual' confidence.[18]

Presumably, however, all that these 'new-found' CBMs had in common was the potential to reduce the risks of war – at a time when public opinion supported such assurances but conventional arms control did not deliver. As CBMs gained prominence, it was natural that the idea would be introduced beyond Europe.

From Europe to the United Nations

In 1979, the United Nations sponsored a meeting of governmental experts to undertake a comprehensive study on confidence-building measures. The study, completed in 1981, noted that while underlying causes of conflicts in many parts of the world had different roots, a major cause of insecurity was a lack of information about the military activities of other states and other matters pertaining to mutual security.[19] The report suggested that implementing measures capable of dispelling possible misunderstanding would help reduce tensions and thus increase confidence and promote more stable relations between states.[20] Another role ascribed to CBMs (and one closely resembling the direction given to the measures in Europe) was to facilitate the process of arms control and disarmament, something in short supply at the time.[21]

Problems of Internationalisation

Although the report's emphasis on the military aspects of CBMs appeared to endorse what was soon termed the 'European model' of confidence-building measures, this was not in fact the case. The issue of universal application provoked controversy, and two main issues surfaced.[22] First, several Third World countries contested the relevance of the European measures to them, arguing that their security concerns were fundamentally different from those of the European states. Threats and threat perceptions outside Europe seldom emanated from outright military conflicts or surprise attacks, but more often from non-traditional security issues, including ethnic, religious, social or economic disputes. Thus, to be relevant, CBMs would have to apply to these areas as well.

Second, most developing countries had very different interpretations of CBMs or, more specifically, of the meaning of 'confidence-building'. Indeed, if the concept advocated by the West emphasised the role of CBMs in eliminating or reducing fears of specific military threats or concerns (such as surprise attack), the developing countries argued that the ultimate purpose of CBMs was to create confidence in the broader sense – international confidence, or mutual confidence between states.

This characterisation of CBMs (which placed great emphasis on terminology and semantics) reinforced the argument that they should be implemented in all sectors of inter-state relations. Indeed, viewed in such broad terms, 'confidence' could not simply emerge from one sector, or be created by military confidence alone.[23]

The problem immediately surfaced of devising non-military measures. The 1981 UN report demonstrated the difficulties (which still exist) of accomplishing such a task. Significantly, the recommendations put forward by the group of experts were not even called CBMs, but 'policies and measures' which could contribute to the building of confidence. Respecting human rights, the sovereignty of states and establishing a new economic order were said to be such policies or measures.[24] The difficulty with this view was that unless these were translated into practice, reiterating generally agreed principles would have little practical effect. As one Western expert noted, 'There is nothing good unless it's being done'.[25]

Thus, as soon as the concept appeared on the international scene, its future was in doubt. This was particularly serious because at the same time, Europe experienced a serious crisis in its CBM practice, which raised considerable doubts about the effectiveness of the 'new' (Western) concept to deal appropriately with a limited number of security concerns.

Confidence-Building Measures in Crisis
Several times during the confrontation between the independent Solidarity trade union and the communist authorities in Poland in 1980–81, the West accused the Soviet Union and its allies of breaching their CSCE CBM obligations. In September 1981, the Soviet Union failed to give proper notification of the largest exercise held by any CSCE state since the signing of the Final Act. The notification of the manoeuvre, code-name *Zapad-81*, did not include the number or the type of troops engaged as specifically required by the Final Act. It did, however, include precise information on the time-frame for the exercise as well as information on its location which, although vague enough to cause other CSCE states to complain, did indicate that the exercise was to take place in the vicinity of Poland.[26] On the eve of the operation, the Soviet newspaper *Izvestiya* reported that the 'exercise' would involve only a 'very limited' number of troops.[27] However, on the second day, the Soviet news agency TASS revealed that 'approximately 100,000 troops' were involved in the manoeuvre.[28]

The incomplete notification of *Zapad-81* was not the first violation of the CBMs. In March and April 1981, the Warsaw Pact failed to give notification of several significant military activities around Poland (*Soyuz-81*); these were severely criticised by the US as 'increasingly menacing troop movements and other threatening activities around Poland'.[29] Finally, the failure to provide notification of the *Soyuz* 'exercises' had been preceded a few months earlier by a particularly vague notification of another large-scale WTO multinational manoeuvre around Poland (*'Bratya po Oruzhiyu'* or *Brotherhood in Arms*, involving 40,000 troops); the time-frame given was the 'first-half of September', and its location described as 'the GDR and adjacent parts of the Baltic'.[30]

What these inadequate notifications suggested (or were actually meant to convey) was unclear. Following the signing of the Final Act in 1975, there were concerns that 'notification according to the CSCE rules could in some circumstances serve to amplify threatening or warning signals'.[31] The Soviets themselves had apparently made the case that 'advance notification of exercises *could* be used to threaten or coerce even without the exercises taking place ... [and that the] signal conveyed would be made more convincing because it would be made under the CSCE arrangements'.[32] 'Whatever the intent', though, as one Western analyst argued, 'the effect was to introduce an unnecessary note of East–West uncertainty into what had otherwise been a relatively unambiguous situation'.[33] In fact, it was later reported that, 'the combination of Soviet military actions and harsh rhetoric, plus an inadequate grasp of what was actually taking place in the border regions around Poland, resulted in US military intelligence issuing an "alert memorandum" contending that [a] Soviet invasion had ... begun'.[34]

Events in Poland clearly demonstrated that CBMs would not deter the Soviet Union from using a display of military force to intimidate, as suggested by the Western concept. Yet, the problem with the CSCE CBMs was greater than just the non-fulfilment of a Western objective. If more information (or transparency) was seen as the obvious way to remove ambiguities and clarify the nature of military activities in Europe, then the information provided by the Warsaw Pact nations under the CBM regime would appear to be at best irrelevant and at worst deceptive.

In fact, the information that the Warsaw Pact states offered in their announcements of impending exercises was often nearly useless – there were few designations for the manoeuvres, numerous vague locations (sometimes only naming a country as the site), some estimated time-frame such as 'beginning of September' and only an approximate number of participating troops (suspiciously, and too often, the number was 25,000 troops, the precise agreed threshold for 'mandatory' reporting under the Helsinki regime).[35] When observers were invited (an exception rather than a rule for the NATO states, who were not invited to Eastern exercises between 1979 and 1985),[36] the restrictions 'not only prevented observers from gaining a clear understanding of the purpose of the manoeuvres, but made it impossible to formulate any realistic appreciation of the tactical capabilities or operational readiness of the troops involved'.[37]

On balance, the impact of the Helsinki CBMs on 'openness' in the Eastern bloc, which NATO had hoped to promote at the CSCE, was also minimal. Of course, it should be recorded that the Eastern states announced forthcoming manoeuvres for the first time, but there was evidence to suggest that even before the CSCE negotiations were concluded, the Soviet Union was actually reducing the amount of information it had previously made public. Military intelligence officers described this at the time as 'an uncustomary silence on the part of the Warsaw Pact nations regarding their manoeuvres'.[38] Following the CBM agreement in Helsinki, it was noted that 'for all practical purposes, Soviet discussions of the system of [Warsaw Pact] joint exercises virtually ceased in 1975'.[39]

It was also noteworthy that while the Eastern states reported no military exercises for five months following the signing of the Final Act, 'reports abounded in the West European press that the Soviets were, in fact, carrying out exercises in excess of 25,000 troops and simply not announcing them'.[40] Later, it was widely believed that the Soviet Union had deliberately adopted the practice of breaking down its exercises into several smaller scale manoeuvres to avoid mandatory reporting.[41]

Given these apparent changes in the Eastern states' exercises and the limited information they provided, it became increasingly difficult to claim that openness was creating more predictability or stability. If anything, the WTO's record of implementation pointed to a false, or deceptive, openness.

Scenarios for a surprise attack obviously never provided a test for CBMs, but it was evident that their potential role in this regard could only have been counter-productive. Not only was no real pattern of WTO manoeuvres emerging, but also, as military analysts pointed out, in any surprise attack the CSCE measures could have been used as a smokescreen. Both the provisions for notification and the invitation of observers could have been manipulated by devising staged exercises in some areas where observers would be invited to testify to a normal peacetime situation; in the meantime, reinforcements could be moved somewhere else – all under the guise of a properly notified manoeuvre.[42]

In the early 1980s, therefore, one could safely say that the concept had reached a dead-end. Ways of developing the 'comprehensive' approach to CBMs as advocated by many non-European countries was not attracting much attention and a final product was considered to be a long way off. In Europe, the practice seemed to be fostering only mistrust as seen in the acrimonious debates at Review Conferences. For the Western states, the experience only confirmed (if confirmation was needed) that the Soviet Union could not, and would not, be trusted; this was a difficult conclusion for those who were suggesting that the application of the Helsinki measures was the first experience based on the concept of 'confidence-building', or that CBMs could improve trust between nations. The only rational conclusion was to require strict verification. At the time, no one believed that the Soviets would accept it (or, if they did, that they would implement it), but then nobody predicted that the Cold War would soon be over.

European Experience Revisited
Soviet President Mikhail Gorbachev's rise to power moved matters along quickly. At the 1986 Stockholm CSCE Conference, the Helsinki CBMs were supplanted by 'second-generation' measures. More comprehensive and with provisions involving mandatory on-site verification, they were renamed confidence- and *security*-building measures (CSBMs).[43] The bold policies initiated by Gorbachev also brought the Cold War to an end. What followed was the continuous development of new CBMs (by then CSBMs) and a steady improvement in implementation.

The fact that this took place between states whose relationship contained more than a residual lack of trust received little notice. Instead, the post-Cold War era celebrated the contribution of the CSCE (and CBMs) in breaking up the East–West and international bipolar Cold War structure. CBMs were promoted as the necessary precursors to the comprehensive and successful arms-control agreements which followed, including the Open Skies and Conventional Armed Forces in Europe (CFE) Treaties.

This led to a revisionist, or selective, re-writing of history. Certainly, the CSCE provided a useful forum for debate which saved time when the situation became ripe for bold initiatives. Yet there was little reason to suggest that the dramatic and positive changes in the Eastern states' policies on CBMs, or on human rights for that matter (another important aspect of the Helsinki Final Act), resulted from the West's repeated attacks at the CSCE meetings, or the acrimonious debate that followed. If anything, the Eastern concessions made on these fronts during the Cold War were just that: concessions – extracted, from time to time, by the West in exchange for compromises sought by the Soviets. In fact, the Conference itself had been the result of such a compromise: the NATO countries (particularly the US) made the opening of the CSCE conditional on Eastern participation in the MBFR talks.[44]

Post-Cold War Developments
The new outlook on the CSCE CBMs only partly accounted for the immense popularity of the concept in the post-Cold War era. While CBMs gained unprecedented recognition in the early 1990s, and the CSCE became an 'inspiration' for others to follow, the European 'model' did not gain acceptance elsewhere. In fact, any discussion of possible lessons or even guidelines from Europe became a politically sensitive subject often associated with 'outside' influence. 'Officially', the main problem with the European approach remained that, with its emphasis on surprise attack and concentration on ground forces, it was too context-dependent. Equally important, as was more forcefully argued after the Cold War, the 'model' (based predominantly on military measures) was not necessarily prone to create 'confidence' in the way that had been advocated since the concept was first introduced internationally in the late 1970s.

Outside Europe, it was argued that to be truly effective CBMs needed to be developed for each region, to take into account the unique situation of each case. In practice, however, this localised approach only appeared to suggest that regional states would decide for themselves what measures (or what combination thereof) they would apply and how. For instance, in areas where maritime aspects play a large role in the security of states, it was suggested that notification of ground troop movements be replaced by notification of naval force movements. In fact, not only did official CBMs practices continue to be predominantly military, with the European measures applied almost *mutatus mutandis*, they were so increasingly often. The only noticeable change in regional approaches has been to rename a disproportionate number of state's initiatives in a wider variety of fields as 'CBMs', or to add 'confidence-building' objectives to an ever-growing number of inter-state activities, and claim this as the development of a confidence-building process.

From Procedure to Process

CBMs are now associated predominantly with a 'confidence-building process'. How this process works in practice is not entirely clear and a general understanding can only be inferred from the few, often-repeated ideas in this context. Central among these is that a confidence-building process contributes to a changing perception of security and information (or transparency) is critical in this regard. Access to accurate information can provide reliable evidence that certain behaviour and actions do not constitute a threat and help to reduce mistrust and misperception. This 'first-hand' information then leads to a gradual, positive reassessment of security perceptions.

Another important idea often voiced in discussion about the CBMs process is that debating, developing, negotiating and implementing CBMs are all integral parts of the confidence-building phenomenon. Consultations and dialogue, for instance, are often depicted as enabling the parties involved to present and explain their views, discuss their positions, expose their goals and motives, and uncover each other's perceptions and interpretations. It is a process which allows participants to become more aware of their respective positions and concerns – and the basis for their actions. The result of these activities is a transformation in thinking, a reassessment of policies and a redefinition of objectives, all of which ultimately lead to the adoption of policies and behaviour mutually profitable to all. Finally, these consultations, meetings and gatherings of top decision-makers, military officials or other influential individuals are also seen as helping to ease tensions and establish an atmosphere of trust, and thus are considered to contribute also to the development of a confidence-building process.

This is a brief analysis of what a 'confidence-building process' means. Most who support such a notion suggest that it involves more than these essential features. Yet the specific elements which constitute, contribute to or trigger a particular confidence-building 'process' are not usually acknowledged. Apart from a 'certainty' that such a process does not simply emerge from the application of specific measures (or from measures applied in the military field only), the idea is perpetually discussed in the abstract.[45] Typical of this thinking is the following comment: 'Confidence-building is a complex and all-encompassing process that aims to create an outcome in which a state will no longer consider another as a threat. As such, CSBMs should also be employed in the economic, political and social fields as well. In this way, we would be better placed to strengthen the understanding between states, and the security situation'.[46]

Such generalities are not particularly illuminating, yet they underscore the dual benefits widely ascribed to the concept since the end of the Cold War, namely that of strengthening security and enhancing understanding between states. The latter dimension, which can be more accurately described as improving cooperation between states, is a key component of the 'new' thinking on CBMs. Indeed, closely associated with the idea of a confidence-building process is the belief that CBMs are useful tools for introducing or developing cooperation between states and that they should be used for this specific purpose.

This belief rests on the premise that states can have relations other than those involving conflict. No matter how hostile or antagonistic a relationship may be, there is always one area of common interest – the avoidance of war. The current outlook on CBMs suggests that once 'cooperation' is established in one field, a foundation then exists for further building. The application of CBMs is strongly believed to produce both a 'spin-off and a 'spill-over' effect. Once a first set of CBM applications exists, more comprehensive undertakings can be developed on the basis of the initial measures. At the same time, other fields and areas of common interests can expand (or, in some cases, reinforce) a developing web of cooperation. These 'vertical' and 'horizontal' impacts not only reinforce one another, but also create their own momentum, producing more common areas of understanding, and mutual interest, more interdependence, cooperation and, of course, confidence.

Competing Ideas or Hybrid Concept?
The shift in emphasis – from enhancing military security to enhancing cooperation – is not without consequences. Preoccupation with developing a process can be criticised for coming at the expense of enhancing security. States which do not trust one another but want reassurance about the peaceful nature of a CBM partner (or the absence of a military threat), need comprehensive agreements with strict implementation. If the purpose of CBMs is seen as more political than military, however, these requirements may be altered so as to avoid making strict demands when the primary purpose is to establish working relationships.

Furthermore, while improving military security and relations between states are not mutually exclusive in that CBMs which enhance security may result in improving relations, attempts to apply the logic in reverse, or only half-way, may not be successful. Undoubtedly, if 'military confidence' is not established (i.e., if security is not assured) there is little likelihood that any overall confidence will develop between two rivals. Also, while 'cooperation' between nations may result from discussions, negotiations or implementations, security will not automatically ensue or be enhanced whenever any measures are being discussed or applied. Yet the current view of CBMs makes no distinction between the two different purposes of application; on the contrary, it sees CBMs as having positive results on both accounts.

New Relevance or Absence of New Ideas?
The resemblance of the 'new' approach to CBMs to that of the 'comprehensive' view put forward by many non-European countries since the late 1970s is striking. The fact that the latter now dominates the European 'model' is not the result of any 'success' story of its own, which would have confirmed the value of its propositions, nor, as suggested above, of any new or clearly defined theoretical framework. The uncertainties of the post-Cold War environment elevated the comprehensive view of CBMs to its current popularity. The perceived usefulness of this approach for dealing with the new international security situation, with its accompanying opportunities and uncertainties, has been reinforced by the lack of innovative or alternative ideas for dealing with the changed circumstances.

Several distinct opportunities surfaced after the Cold War to resolve specific protracted conflicts. Entire regions seemed more open to replace confrontation with cooperation, or at least to work towards the latter. At a time when friends and foes are not clearly identified, CBMs provide a useful framework for a cautious course of action. Initiating, or developing, a security dialogue based on confidence-building measures is seen as a low-cost tactic which brings potential adversaries together to talk about security concerns. Such dialogue can help create new principles, or rules to regulate the military behaviour of states. They can also establish habits of cooperation. When CBMs are in place, they help reduce the risks of conflicts.

The end of the Cold War has also increased attention on so-called 'new' potential flash-points, where long-time enemies remain on the verge of conflict. For those relationships where the 'enemy-image' is a prominent feature, the main usefulness of CBMs is seen in reverse. Although their primary importance is for avoiding wars, these measures are used increasingly to break deadlocked situations and improve inter-state relations. Whether CBMs can deliver in all situations, or be successful when used to enhance security *and* cooperation simultaneously remains to be seen.

The Contemporary Case for CBMs

After extensive evolution of the concepts, the most widely acknowledged value of CBMs is that they help avoid wars and promote peaceful relations. There are a number of ways in which CBMs are said to fulfil these goals.

The risks of war can be decreased by reducing misunderstanding and misinterpretation. Because military activities are inherently ambiguous, they can easily be misinterpreted. A routine military training exercise, for instance, can be mistaken by another state as an offensive action and trigger an undesirable reaction, leading to unintended conflict. Advance notification of military activities, however, can avert such scenarios, allowing states to avoid a possible misinterpretation of intended peaceful purposes. This assumes particular significance where routine activity is carried out during a crisis, as it offers confirmation at a time of great tension that the events are not related.

Besides increasing understanding of the pattern of routine military activities, advance notification is also important for increasing predictability and promoting stability. By reducing apprehensions, fears, suspicions and tensions, it can also increase trust and build confidence.

Observing military activities can also play a useful role in reducing the risks of misunderstanding or miscalculation, by allowing all parties the opportunity to confirm the accuracy of information previously given. In theory, observation also provides reassurance that the activities are carried out in a non-aggressive manner and are peaceful in nature.

In addition to information about military activities, including advance notification, exchanging basic facts about military facilities, structures and budgets can help reduce mistrust and misunderstanding. Information about major weapon systems, weapon inventories, planned procurement or weapon transfers are all believed to be beneficial in reducing the excessive and destabilising acquisition of weapons, preventing an arms race and facilitating disarmament.

Increasing transparency in military matters lies at the core of the confidence-building approach. The lack of information about matters related to defence policies or armaments, for example, is strongly believed to create mistrust and tensions. Secrecy breeds suspicions, and when states do not communicate, or there is a lack of information about other states' military capabilities or activities, officials tend to make worst case analyses.

The importance given to the benefits of exchanging or acquiring raw information, stems from the expectation that once information is made public, it can be clarified. In this regard, another important aspect of CBMs is establishing regular contacts and consultations between military and defence officials to discuss weapon acquisitions, troop activities and structures, military doctrines, security concepts or security concerns. Such regular exchanges of views between representatives involved in military planning are thought to contribute to greater mutual understanding, especially by providing better knowledge of the intentions guiding the activities or structures of armed forces. These exchanges not only clarify, but can also help resolve problems.

Another value of CBMs is in establishing principles, rules, norms or standard of conduct regulating states' behaviour. At a general level, most CBM applications are deemed useful by making the behaviour of states more predictable. In this latter respect, most CBMs are also seen as helping to stabilise inter-state relations by making them more orderly. Over time, such an application could become a standard against which any deviation may be judged unlawful, thus contributing to the creation of new rules of behaviour in states relations. By requesting that forces operating in close proximity to one another conduct their operations in a manner designed to reduce the risks of war, such a code of conduct is expected to have an immediate and beneficial impact.

Mutual restraints on certain military activities, or constraints on their operations, are particularly important for reducing the risks of conflict and promoting better relations. Limiting the number or scope of the most potentially threatening military activities removes grounds for possible conflicts. Prohibiting activities in areas of tensions also removes the risk of pre-emptive actions. Limiting, constraining or prohibiting activities are, however, usually reserved for a second stage of application, after more modest measures have been tried.

All of the above are believed to create an atmosphere conducive to achieving the major goals of CBMs, including arms control and disarmament. These expectations, as well as the measures on which they are based, require that the CBM partners have no intention of using force against one another, and that their actions are indeed only peaceful. It also points to the fact that the security perceptions to be changed by applying CBMs are indeed only misperceptions to begin with.

The concept of confidence-building measures is clearly still evolving. While no formal theory exists, its development has worked like a magnet. Many potentially beneficial roles have been ascribed to the measures, and few have been discarded. This, it seems, explains the current uncritical search for CBMs, as well as the existence of the dual benefits ascribed to the process. Indeed, while the existing application and recommendations continue to be made for the military field, it is usually unclear whether these measures are seen primarily as security-enhancing tools or as a mechanism, part of a larger process, to work towards less antagonistic relations.

Yet, whether CBMs are favoured as simple measures to address specific security/military concerns, or as part of a larger process to improve relations between states, the concept relies essentially on applying certain specific measures. Indeed, even if the process of building confidence is believed to be more significant than the application of simple measures, the discussions and exchanges on the issue (believed by many to be an integral part of the process) ultimately aim for some measures to be negotiated and applied. This, however, is not an easy task.

II. NEGOTIABILITY VERSUS NEGOTIATIONS

Confidence is necessary to develop and maintain peace. To suggest that the CBM tools, or the confidence-building approach, can succeed where other methods flounder, is not so clear. The obstacles to applying CBMs effectively are many and varied. Some stem from the negotiating process, the CBMs chosen and the players involved; others can be found in the design and implementation of the agreements, while many derive from the concept's most basic assumptions.

At present, the vast interest in CBMs stems not only from the intrinsic security/military value ascribed to the measures, or from the expectations of improved relationships associated with development of a process, but from the strong belief that CBMs are easy to negotiate. In that respect, there are a number of basic characteristics of a CBM approach that are believed to influence nations to participate, and as participation increases so does the chance that some will be successful.

Negotiability: The Political Attractiveness of CBMs

Proponents suggest that at least four factors facilitate consideration of CBMs, even by the most hostile parties. These measures require only a minimum of political will, they imply reciprocity, they are initially non-constraining and they involve no legally binding obligations.

Minimum Political Will

As the primary focus of CBMs is not to resolve disputes between states, giving them due consideration requires only a minimum of political will. For many national authorities, this presents a double advantage – one relates to their external position, and the other deals with internal considerations.

There are numerous reasons why the root causes of a security problem between rival states are not, or cannot be, considered. One of the parties may not be willing to address the issue, another may not recognise the need to resolve it, or one or more of the parties may not be able or ready to do so. Alternatively, there may be no short term solution because of conflicting interests that are unlikely to change. Furthermore, even in situations where one of the parties might be interested in addressing the problem, fear of compromising or signalling a position of weakness can deter them from making an overture, resulting in a lost opportunity.

Whatever reasons prevent movement on core issues, advocates point out that by leaving aside the most divisive ones, CBMs remove a significant obstacle to discussions while offering the possibility of establishing a dialogue between rivals. Depending on the level of acrimony or hostility between parties, the aim of such dialogue may simply be to preclude certain situations from erupting into conflicts, to prevent the overall relationship from deteriorating or to improve its prospects.

If CBMs can allow 'something' to be done while not compromising any one position, they can be similarly valuable for dealing with difficult internal situations. Domestically, resolving a conflict with an adversary may not be popular and can be the greatest obstacle to progress towards more peaceful relations. A number of interest groups, political parties or institutions may find their legitimacy or prestige threatened by the resolution of the issue and work to prevent or undermine any process of accommodation. Even when national authorities are limited from taking bold steps, CBMs provide a tool for doing 'something'. This is especially true if the CBM agenda only relates to steps for avoiding possible 'accidental' wars. Few national groups want to be seen as so obstructive that they openly disapprove of measures to prevent 'unwanted' wars, or want to risk being held responsible for any conflict which might erupt from an uncontrolled situation or accident. This, of course, also holds true for inter-state dialogue as, to borrow from Soviet rhetoric, all states want to be seen as 'peace-loving' nations.

Reciprocity

A second important characteristic of CBMs is their reciprocal nature. As a way to preserve or increase one own's security, unilateral initiatives are rarely the favoured first option. In general, governments shy away from the idea that unilateral action can encourage reciprocal action by the other side, as there is always the risk that self-imposed restraint will not be matched. 'Negotiated security', in contrast, ensures that whatever steps or undertakings are taken will be reciprocated. Negotiated agreements usually impose equal or similar obligations on all parties, as the only way to obtain concession from one side is for the other to accept similar compromises or limitations. In short, the undertaking does not require any of the parties to accept more than the others. The issue of reciprocity is particularly important for states with no history of cooperation with one another and who do not trust each other.

Lack of Constraint

Another attractive feature of CBMs is that they initially do not entail significant undertakings. By definition, CBMs are meant to begin with modest measures, often relating only to the exchange of information and personnel. As the concept is proposed, only the full and comprehensive implementation of initial modest measures can create the necessary confidence for negotiating more stringent ones. At the outset states will not want to commit to far-reaching or demanding projects. Thus, in the first stage, CBMs do not affect the structure or levels of military forces, nor do they attempt to constrain military power in any way. Instead, they focus on clarifying the military and political intentions of the parties.

The modest, non-constraining nature of CBMs means that, if need be, commitments can be quickly revoked without any significant or permanent loss as would be the case, for instance, in reducing manpower or destroying weapon systems. It is also widely believed that the simplicity of most CBM projects allows progress to be made quickly, because they exclude many of the political, organisational or technical problems associated with other initiatives.

The Degree of Obligation

An important aspect of CBMs is their juridical status. Although a number of treaties are depicted as having a confidence-building effect, CBM negotiations are seldom undertaken for the purpose of signing a treaty. This may come at a later stage, but in general, CBMs arrangements begin with voluntary or so-called 'politically binding' arrangements. This does not mean that all or even a majority of these types of agreements explicitly state such a fact, but it is a generally agreed principle, and also reflected in practice.

This specific feature of CBM agreements probably derives from the initial European experience whereby, in accordance with the desire of its signatories, the Helsinki Final Act was not a legally binding document eligible for registration as a treaty or international agreement under Article 102 of the United Nations Charter. Nevertheless, the participating states generally accepted that by signing the Final Act, they were making a solemn political commitment to fulfil the declared intentions. As was soon discovered, however, not all CSCE signatories had the same interpretation of these 'solemn' declarations. In order to increase commitment and obtain a greater degree of uniformity in applying these measures (which was also compromised by the use of distinct formulations in the document that reportedly signified different levels of obligations), the NATO states called for the CBMs to be made 'politically binding'.

While the precise meaning and implications of the term 'politically binding' remain unclear, it is often noted that a number of advantages ensue from avoiding agreements in a formal treaty, not least of which is that states may more readily accept voluntary agreements. Avoiding legal agreements allows legal complications to be averted, such as the ratification process which can be complicated. It also helps circumvent complex language formulations usually associated with the drafting of treaties, which can also prolong discussions. Another advantage in choosing a non-legalistic approach is that states can avoid commitments that they may rather not have to keep in the future.

Choosing CBMs? Attractiveness Revisited
Given the way that CBMs are presented as low-cost, low-risk measures, it is easy to understand why proponents believe they would easily be accepted by most nations. This, however, is not the case. Regardless of the political viability or negotiability ascribed to CBMs, their relative acceptability and feasibility are greatly overrated, as other factors will influence, and very often deter, a government's willingness to adopt such measures.

Cost/Benefit Analysis
At a general level, common threats or shared dangers motivate states to collaborate. In many regions today, threat perceptions are relatively low and there is no recognised external common enemy to act as a catalyst in motivating states to participate in cooperative agreements. Furthermore, experience suggests that even where the potential for conflict is acute (and may be recognised as such by the concerned parties), there is no automatic assurance that CBMs will be applied. Reviewing the US–Soviet record of negotiations during the Cold War, Barry Blechman noted that despite the enormous and significant dangers the 'resorting to force' option carried in the relationship between the two great nuclear powers, there were relatively few agreements to avoid accidental war. One interesting point applicable to a number of existing situations, was that the concerned parties did not share the same assessment of the most probable causes of war. As Blechman noted, 'It is not that the Soviets do not understand the technical risks that these measures are intended to reduce. They simply attribute far less importance to them among the complex of factors that might lead to a war than would many

Americans'.[1] Furthermore, the Soviets probably did not 'believe that such technical arrangements would be particularly important in reducing nuclear dangers'.[2]

Shared dangers are no guarantee of shared interests in reducing those dangers. Blechman recognised the absence of such a direct correlation when, referring to the superpowers' CBM dialogue again, he noted that 'the Soviets probably perceive[d] some benefit in the continuance of public concerns about the danger of nuclear war'.[3] Even more disturbing for those who believe that discussions of 'cooperative' measures (like CBMs) automatically imply some sort of 'cooperative' behaviour, Blechman noted that the Soviets probably wished 'to avoid concluding agreements that might serve to ease public concerns about nuclear war and, thus, pressure Western leaders to make concessions in other arms talks'.[4]

While this is possibly an extreme example, it certainly points out some of the difficulties inherent in CBM negotiations. Stronger states, for instance, may have less interest in such agreements. With superior military might they may be confident of deterring a crisis from erupting or, if a crisis did occur, of controlling its effects.

Mutual interest is another important factor for cooperation, although it does not necessarily mean automatic endorsement of CBMs. Notwithstanding possible misgivings about the usefulness of certain measures, as in the Soviet case noted above, national leaders will always weigh the measures against the *status quo* before committing to an agreement. In other words, an agreement will have to present greater advantages than the costs of doing nothing at all. Unless states want a change in the existing situation, it may be difficult to obtain cooperation 'for the sake' of cooperation, no matter how low the costs may be. The impact of the Cold War's demise on international politics has not triggered a universal transformation of attitudes in this regard.

Overall, however, the difficulties of defining and identifying the existence of common threats and dangers may be the greatest mitigating factor against expanded use of CBMs. Mexico's comments at a 1994 'Meeting of Experts on CBMs', convened to identify relevant CBMs for the Organisation of American States (OAS), are particularly note-worthy. Mexico had 'some problems with the Meeting's approach to its topic, because it is proceeding to draw up a list, or catalogue, of military confidence-building measures without having previously identified the military threats that must be reduced or neutralized'.[5] As further noted, 'The sensitive nature and importance of our work requires ... that we identify which threats we want to prevent, so as to devise specific measures to counteract current or potential threats'.[6] Certainly, the Latin American case is not unique in the post-Cold War era. Still, to complicate matters further, the perception of potential risks of conflict is relatively low in many areas. Probably representing a common view held by ASEAN countries and in the Asia-Pacific region in general, the Deputy Foreign Minister of Malaysia pointed out, 'We may have problems, but they are not that serious to result in confrontation or war ... we do not at any time ever envisage that we should act tough and use military means to solve our problems with our neighbours'.[7]

Challenging the view that the absence of external threats or low perceptions of potential conflicts can hinder, postpone or preclude CBMs, proponents of the approach point out that, like common security, CBMs are 'predicated on the assumption that interests between member states may be divergent and that there is always the possibility of conflict – including armed conflict – emerging between them. CSBM regimes are intended to minimise the chances of such conflicts escalating to the level of violent confrontation'.[8] Taking this point a step further, and using ASEAN as an example, 'The fact that ASEAN confronts no external threat is thus no argument against creating a sub-regional (ASEAN-based) CSBM security community'.[9] This may very well be the case, but the fact that CBMs *may* be relevant in many places does not mean that they *will* be employed.

Who Proposes and What?
CBM advocates often point out that the advantage of this approach is that all states can participate in implementation. Yet CBMs do not always (if ever) affect states in the same manner. Furthermore, proposals will not be viewed in the same way by all participants.

Regarding the Korean peninsula, one analyst recalled, 'North and South Korean arms control experts have each noted the similarity of the other's proposals to create a genuine demilitarised zone along the border between North and South. One North Korean scholar noted, however, that the South invariably rejected the North's proposals and vice versa – not withstanding their similarity'.[10] While other issues certainly contributed to the mutual rejection of these initiatives, the Korean case underscores the point that states may be reluctant to believe that propositions by former enemies or potential rivals are put forward in good faith.

Proposals by major regional powers can also represent a problem for they are more likely to be seen as attempts to influence or dominate the political/military landscape of a region. This has been noted repeatedly in Latin America where recommendations put forward by the US have been viewed as 'suspect', or having a hidden agenda. More specifically, US proposals for furthering cooperation against drug-trafficking (discussed in the Latin American context as a new type of CBMs) have been perceived by a number of countries as bordering on interference in their internal affairs. Several national military establishments also resent what they see as attempts to diminish the role of the local armed forces by transforming them into simple police forces.

Even proposals emanating from the same region, if put forward by a dominant power, can receive a similar negative response. In Latin America, Brazil sees US proposals as a way to further US hegemonic ambitions, while Brazilian proposals for the region are viewed by neighbouring states with similar suspicions.

Asymmetry in Capacity

If disparity in the size, resources, population or military capacity of countries creates a sense of insecurity in many areas, it can also represent a formidable obstacle to developing CBMs. As a Chilean General noted, 'The sensation of mistrust will always be felt more strongly by the weaker party to a conflict .... [and] confidence-building measures may heighten the weaker nation's sense of defencelessness. To avert these perceptions, CBMs must be designed in such a way as to provide real reductions in tension, demanding more of the party claiming superiority to ensure adequate balance. This goal, however, appears to be unrealistic; no nation will agree to reduce its capabilities further than its opponent'.[11]

If engaging the participation of smaller states poses a challenge to the development of CBMs, respecting the security interests of those states as participants in larger, or region-wide, regimes can also add further complications. This has been seen on several occasions in Europe. At the 1977 Belgrade CSCE Review Conference, for instance, Western states proposed that the threshold for notification of large military manoeuvres in Europe should be reduced from 25,000 troops (the Helsinki-agreed parameter) to 10,000 troops. Although the Neutral and Non-aligned (NNA) nations had been the most enthusiastic partisans of CBMs in the CSCE (often suggesting going beyond simple notification and proposing placing limits on military activities), they opposed the Western notification proposal. Switzerland, in particular, strongly objected to the measure, claiming that given the size of its army and the way it operated, the notification of manoeuvres at such a low level would be discriminatory.[12] Almost ten years later, at the 1984–86 Stockholm Conference, NATO proposed that the CSCE participating states agree to give notification of mobilisation activities. Considered one of the most destabilising and potentially dangerous military activities a nation could undertake, the measure, if implemented, would have greatly improved the effectiveness of the CBM system.[13] Again, however, and despite their continued strong commitment to the CBM regime, members of the NNA group opposed the measure, arguing that in view of their heavy reliance on mobilisation it would prejudice and weaken their defences.[14]

Area of Application and Choice of Participants
Defining a geographical area, or deciding on CBM partners, can also impede successful negotiation. The best illustration of the difficulties raised by these two issues (which are often intertwined) can probably be found in the Asia-Pacific region, and most particularly in the newly established ASEAN Regional Forum (ARF). Created in 1994, the ARF has been hailed as 'the first ever "official" Asia-Pacific forum dedicated to security issues', with great expectations for extensive CBMs application.[15] Drawing its membership from almost 20 nations, the ARF avoided imposing geographical limits to membership.[16] As one official explained, 'Even if such a straightforward criterion as the geographical delimitation of the Asia-Pacific region was used, questions would inevitably arise with the application of such criterion. Would it correspond to the geographical outline of APEC [Asia-Pacific Economic Cooperation] (with the exception of Taiwan)? Or is it to cover the area loosely defined as East Asia and the North Pacific? Or should the geographical definition reflect the distribution of security interests'?[17] Each of these options has different implications including, if the APEC one was chosen, broadening the ARF's scope of application to some Latin American countries.

'For the time being, the eligibility for membership in ... [the] ARF has been based on political decisions, that is, eligible members are those that have formal relations with ASEAN'.[18] While such criteria do not help resolve the issue of geographical demarcation, they have the 'advantage' of justifying the fact that, following the opposition of China, Taiwan had been excluded from participating in the Forum.[19] Such exclusion, however, clearly contradicts the contention that 'for ... [the] ARF to maintain a sense of security among its regional partners, ASEAN members strongly feel that it should operate ... on ... the principle of inclusiveness in terms of membership'.[20] Furthermore, it also raises doubts about the Forum's ability to fulfil its main objective of maintaining and securing peace throughout the region. Indeed, serious security implications ensue from the two-China situation. Another important source of tension in the region which could degenerate into open confrontation is the conflicting claims to the Spratly Islands in the South China Sea. This conflict involves no less than six countries, and Taiwan is the only nation with claims to some of the islands *not* to be included in the Forum.

A completely different issue arising from the question of participation and the area of application relates to the fact that like security, security threats and perception of threats, the effects of applying CBMs do not necessarily respect borders. Examples of problems resulting from this issue can again be found in the ARF experience. In late 1995, the ASEAN member-states signed the South-east Asian Nuclear Weapons Free Zone Treaty. Although nuclear-weapon free zones (NWFZ) are recognised worldwide as important confidence-building measures, the small ASEAN nations' attempt to establish such a zone in South-east Asia was immediately criticised by the US and China. The US was said to fear that the Treaty could restrain the operation of its nuclear-powered, or nuclear-armed ships and aircraft which often transit through the area. China criticised the agreement on the ground that its geographical scope included parts of the South China Sea, in which Beijing has numerous territorial disputes with the other ASEAN nations.[21] Paradoxically, both China and the US participate in the ARF group that the ASEAN states have helped established. The disagreement between the smaller ASEAN nations and two of their dialogue partners in the larger ASEAN Regional Forum raises further doubts about the Forum's capacity to deal effectively with security issues in the region.

The area of application and the choice of CBM partners can be sufficient to abort even the best intentioned proposals. This seems to have been the case in the 1990s with the failed efforts by several European and other governments to establish a Conference on Security and Cooperation in the Mediterranean (CSCM) and the Middle East , similar to the CSCE and with some of its original CBMs.[22] Indeed, while US participation was considered imperative to the success of the enterprise, Washington showed little interest in being brought into a process which also sought to involve countries like Iran, Iraq, Syria and Libya. This does not even take into account whether all (or any) of these same countries would have agreed to participate in a forum which would, at least in principle, also include Israel – and vice-versa, of course.

What CBMs First?

Parties' preference as to what, or what type of, CBMs should be discussed initially can be another major stumbling block preventing negotiations from ever reaching the serious stage. The dialogue between the two Koreas provides a vivid example. In 1996, the South Koreans not only insisted on negotiating a number of non-military CBMs, but believed that these political measures, along with some military (but non-constraining) CBMs should precede discussion on arms reductions. In clear contrast, the North Koreans demanded that constraints on military activities be the first priority, while clearly emphasising that CBMs without arms control would be impossible. The significance each side attaches to its own negotiating priority is such that 'South Korean officials have dismissed most North Korean proposals not based on the build-up of trust and confidence-building measures as unrealistic and propagandist'.[23]

The Type of CBMs

The type of CBMs proposed for negotiations can certainly constitute the greatest obstacle to beginning discussion or reaching agreement. Indeed, contrary to popular belief, CBMs do not necessarily bring benefits (or the same benefits) to all nations. As noted by several observers, while CBMs are applied symmetrically, their impact is often asymmetrical.[24] Several examples illustrate this point.

First, dissimilarity in geopolitical or strategic interests can result in measures being advanced that clearly benefit one side over the other. In the US–Soviet proposals, the US was always inclined to propose land measures while the Soviets favoured maritime ones, reflecting the fact that the former was a more sea-dependent power and the latter a land power. Similarly, suggestions made by some Arab nations for CBMs to be applied in the nuclear field would certainly, given Israel's reported unmatched capabilities in this field, affect Tel Aviv more than the Arab nations themselves.

Another type of asymmetrical impact ensuing from CBM application relates to measures which, although appearing fair and acceptable to all, would have more profound implications for some nations than others. Revealing information on military budgets, defence expenditures, troop strength, structure of the armed forces and the like is a case in point for states where secrecy is part of the fabric of society and where ruling regimes can be directly threatened by greater openness. Transparency for weaker or smaller states, or for those not belonging to any military alliances or collective security systems, can also raise issues of vulnerability which may not be felt by others.

The asymmetrical effects of CBMs can also emanate from specific parameters or details of proposals which, although they appear fair to all parties, would in fact have a greater impact on one side. One example taken from the CSCE experience was the Soviet proposals banning all military manoeuvres above a level of 40,000–60,000 troops.[25] For several reasons, including the fact that NATO's membership was almost double that of the Warsaw Pact, the Western Alliance needed to hold exercises involving a much larger number of troops than its Eastern counterpart.[26]

Similarly, even the most modest and non-controversial measures can have an important or unacceptable asymmetrical impact depending on the specific parameters set. The 1993 United Nations Register of Conventional Arms only covers imports and exports of seven categories of conventional arms. Not included are domestic arms production and military holdings. As a result, 'countries participating in the Register that rely heavily on imports have accepted greater transparency in their overall arms procurement than participating states that produce many of their own arms'.[27] While the UN is committed to reviewing this issue, failure to resolve this 'inequality' quickly has already resulted in countries withdrawing from the Register. Egypt, for one, has officially declared that this was one of the main reasons it decided to opt out of the regime in 1994, only one year after its establishment.[28]

Intricacies of Negotiations
As illustrated above, the acceptability of CBMs cannot, and should not, be taken for granted. CBMs are not the easy, 'cost-free' enterprises so often described, and interesting states in discussing them is not necessarily an easy task. Yet, while reaching consensus on the precise content of such a dialogue can entail protracted discussions on a topic which may never materialise, other considerations can come in the way of negotiated agreements. These can be better appreciated by considering some of the problems associated with formal negotiations, problems which are likely to be high on the 'cost/benefit' analysis that most national authorities would make before deciding to participate in any CBM regime.

Getting on with Negotiations?
Entering into negotiations always implies taking risks – risks of being trapped, risks of having more demands made, risks of failures.[29]. In the

34

early 1980s, India was one of the staunchest opponents of CBMs. Believing that the 'new' concept was just another ploy by the developed nations to limit the military potential of developing countries, Delhi feared accepting simple CBMs would lead to demands for verification of its military power.[30]

The US Navy has also expressed concern that negotiating naval CBMs might be the beginning of a 'slippery slope' leading to constraints and reductions.[31] Similar fears have been attributed to China as a possible explanation for its reluctance to discuss the application of such measures in Asia.[32]

Tokyo and Moscow have had first-hand experience of the effects that pre-negotiations carried out in public can have on raising false expectations. As one observer recalled of the 1991 Japanese–Soviet summit meeting, 'Despite widespread press reports that an array of agreements and CBMs would be finalised, the results were disappointing'.[33]

While these concerns may be sufficient for some states to reject or postpone involvement with confidence-building measures, they represent only one aspect of formal CBM negotiations which could deter consideration of this approach, or which could impede mutually agreed measures.

Mixed Motives

Much as with any international political negotiation, it cannot be assumed that states enter CBMs negotiations for a single reason, or that their primary motivation is concluding an agreement. It may be the predominant objective, but there are usually others as well.

In examining some of the motives for entering into arms-control negotiations during the Cold War, Michael Sheehan noted:

> [While there might be] a desire to conclude an agreement ... a state may seek to give the impression that this is its objective when in fact there are other reasons. These may include using the talks as a propaganda platform, exploring the adversary's attitudes and possibly obtaining useful intelligence gains, diverting public attention from domestic difficulties or international setbacks in other areas, wishing to deceive the adversary as to the depths of one's animosity or to delay certain political developments by making progress on them a hostage to the fortune of progress in the negotiations.[34]

Uncovering any of these motives can detract governments from considering or pursuing a CBM process – especially if the potential risks involved outweigh the perceived benefits of a negotiated agreement.

Tactics
As pursuing motives other than CBMs cannot be ruled out from negotiations (but would more likely be a question of scope and degree, differing in each case), it is probable that parties involved will use various tactics to protect or advance their interests. There is indeed no reason to believe that considerations of national interest will be eliminated simply because the subject of discussion is CBMs. In fact, examples of all of the above abound in the international track-record of CBM discussions and negotiations.

Conflicting Interests
The case of the US–USSR, land versus sea, proposals has already been discussed in the context of differing geopolitical or strategic interests resulting in a 'one-sided' proposal. Yet to suggest that this is the only reason why each superpower continuously pursued agreement on measures which would have had a greater impact on the other side would be missing an important point, namely that a prominent purpose for advancing such measures was precisely to constrain the power of the other side.[35]

Certainly, many proposals put forward in the CSCE negotiations were clearly formulated to gain unilateral advantage. The Soviet Union, for example, repeatedly used the European forum to advance schemes that were either for propaganda purposes or to benefit its position. These two motives were certainly predominant in the repeated calls for a ban on large military manoeuvres exceeding a level of 40,000–60,000 troops which, as explained above, would have affected NATO much more than the Warsaw Pact.

From the other perspective, however, most of NATO's proposals were equally one-sided. The Western states actually conceded very little at Helsinki by requesting the notification of large military manoeuvres. Indeed, 'given the population and industrial density of Western Europe, large scale military exercises [had to] be planned far in advance and adequate notification given to the civil authorities and population to ensure a minimum of disruption to both the civilian sector and the military exercise taking place'.[36] Furthermore, the information provided in the Western notification was 'not substantially different from that made public prior to the Helsinki Agreement'.[37] Surprisingly, even the small NNA nations did not escape harsh criticism; one Western participant to the Stockholm Conference described some of their positions as 'hypocrisy'.[38]

Similarly, it has been suggested that in the context of the Middle East peace process, Egypt's insistence (supported by other Arab states) on opening the security dialogue with the issue of nuclear weapons had a strong propaganda purpose; on the eve of the 1995 Nuclear Non-proliferation Treaty Review and Extension Conference, Egypt was trying to maximise pressure on Israel to sign the Treaty. On the other hand, Israeli insistence that non-nuclear CBMs be discussed and fully implemented before agreeing to negotiate the nuclear issue has been seen as an attempt to postpone discussion of the latter *sine die*.

Finally, in South Asia, India and Pakistan initiated an important CBM dialogue in 1990, and have attempted to use the negotiating process to broaden the scope of discussion to include other issues, such as Kashmir.[39] There have also been attempts to make the continuation of the CBM dialogue conditional on progress on these issues. As a result of these tactics, no high-level official meetings to discuss CBMs have been held since January 1994.[40]

The above examples are not to suggest that all proposals are put forward solely to gain advantage at the expense of other participant(s), but to highlight the point that negotiating CBMs does not preclude pursuing a variety of other goals, nor are they necessarily motivated by a single reason. Nor do the above examples suggest that there was a lack of real security concerns underlying the different negotiating behaviour of the participants. On the contrary, they emphasise such concerns. Thus, the analysis of CBM negotiations underscores the fact that whether or not the overall objective is to conclude so-called 'coopera-tive' agreements, states' *self*-interests remain the primary criteria against which to judge the acceptability of any measure, while conflicting national interests cannot be excluded from the process – something too often neglected when advertising the simplicity of CBMs.

Negotiating Outcome and CBM Design
Although a variety of factors can limit the number of agreements, these impediments do not rule out the possibility that some measures will be successfully negotiated. As the final outcome of this process and the basis upon which a state will reassure and convince other partners of its peaceful intentions, the scope and nature of CBM agreements are of

great significance. While the concrete results of every negotiation differ, any survey of standard agreements is bound to highlight three main weaknesses in the design of initial arrangements: the ambiguous nature of the level of obligation, the vague formulation of many stipulations and the absence of verification provisions.

Level of Commitment/Degree of Obligation

Any CBM proposal can, if agreed upon, be registered in many ways. As a general rule, when parties definitely intend to bind themselves to certain obligations, they adopt formulations and procedures to be governed by the Law of Treaties.[41] Treaties represent the most formal kind of agreements between states and imply the highest degree of obligation for compliance. Legal consequences also flow from a treaty. This is not the case with voluntary and 'politically binding' arrangements, and no legal consequences ensue from non-compliance with such undertakings. Furthermore, the degree of obligation implied in 'politically-binding' agreements is ambiguous, and it is difficult to ascertain an intermediary level of obligation between a voluntary commitment and a politically binding undertaking. Are 'politically binding' measures more than voluntary but less than mandatory? Are voluntary measures only guidelines or recommendations, which may or may not entail definite actions? More importantly, do these different categories confer, or actually involve, different levels of obligation, degrees of commitment and responsibility, different rules or standards of application, or different expectations about compliance? If so, are these readily recognisable by the parties and, more significantly, will all CBM partners interpret them in the same manner? If the arrangements are not registered in a binding legal document and, thus, cannot be amended in treaty form, does it mean that any communiqué or declaration issued after the signing can (unilaterally) alter contents or applications?

In short, while 'voluntarism' may be implicit in any instrument which is not intended to be legally binding, far less evident is what precisely is expected from voluntary and politically-binding arrangements, and how the latter differ from the former. Political commitments will obviously always be subject to interpretation by national authorities. Yet by purposely suggesting varying but undefined 'degrees' of commitments, ambiguity is introduced, allowing for interpretation based on 'degrees' of obligations; this is certainly not the most useful characteristic of an exercise designed to dispel misperceptions and misinterpretations.

On a more abstract level, the lack of legal status and clarity regarding the binding force of the arrangements suggests a reluctance to complete commitment, if not 'a lack of seriousness', for the enterprise.[42] If treaty status is reserved for formal agreements, does this imply that others are less formal or important? As John Borawski observed in his study on the legal dimensions of the CSCE CBMs, 'a legal obligation conveys the highest sense of obligation ... which a political pledge does not match'.[43] Furthermore, 'Despite use of the phrase "politically binding," it is difficult to believe that states will regard their obligations as seriously as if the CBMs were codified in an international agreement'.[44] Of more consequential effect, perhaps, one security analyst also pointed out in reference to the voluntary nature of the initial CSCE CBMs that, 'by forswearing pretences of legality, they foster a certain continuing skepticism ... and thus tend to lower expectations of the extent to which they can be relied upon'.[45]

Vague Stipulations
Certainly the problem of ambiguous 'degrees' of obligation and uncertain commitments could be addressed (or redressed) in the actual agreements. Yet judging by those which have been made public (not a golden rule for CBMs – and certainly another paradox of an exercise predominantly concerned with increasing transparency), this is not the case.

Usually standard CBM agreements are relatively bare in details; most do not specify any time-frame for the agreement to remain in force nor do they include denunciation clauses or stipulations about the circumstances in which withdrawal would be permitted (or would be considered justified). Also, they do not always contain procedures for reviewing problems which may arise from implementation. Moreover, rather than clarifying issues of ambiguity in obligations, the texts of agreements often seem to compound the problem by using mostly vague or non-committal language to describe the 'obligations' of states.

One such example is the 1991 Agreement Between Pakistan and India on Advance Notice on Military Exercises, Manoeuvres and Troops Movements. After noting in the preamble 'the need' for advance notification, Article I stipulates that both governments have decided that 'their Land, Naval and Air Forces *will avoid* holding military man-oeuvres and exercises in close proximity to each other'.[46] How this 'neither will/neither won't' statement should be practised is unclear, but is certainly open to differing interpretation by both parties.

Article 6 of the same Agreement covers the type of information to be included in the notification of major exercises. It is written in a such a way that it is difficult to know if any information will ever be provided, or even needs to be given at all. The stipulation in this regard simply notes that the 'information ... will be *intimated*'.

Finally, Article 8, dealing with certain special concentrations of troops not covered by other provisions, stipulates that these concentrations 'will be notified to the other side at least two days before the start of their movements, *whenever possible*'. The obligations involved here are even more difficult to ascertain as it is not entirely clear, for instance, whether the formulation '*whenever possible*' refers to the two days' advance notice, or to the issuance of the notification itself. Only further reading of the Article illuminates the matter, as the next sentence notes, 'In case of immediate movements, information *may* be passed on Hot Line to the Army Headquarters of the other country', thus clarifying somewhat that the '*whenever possible*' applies to the two days' notice. Whether such notification will ever be transmitted, however, is questionable because the only procedure noted regarding such a transmission is that of the hot line, and the use of the phrase '*may* be passed on the Hot Line', rather than a much more decisive and precise formulation like '*will* be passed', raises doubts on the matter.

Absence of Verification
The lack of verification provisions common to most 'first-generation' agreements is a third standard design feature that has drawbacks. Not all CBMs, of course, can be verified. Yet, for those which can be, the absence of any such mechanism (or, as prevailing thinking suggests, withholding verification until a second and more advanced stage of application) is an important weakness. The main purposes of verification are to ascertain compliance with an agreement and to deter possible violations. On a general level, the non-verifiability of arrangements can add to the problem of low commitment by dismissing an important guarantee of compliance, which could also demonstrate how much importance the parties attached to the exercise.

In the absence of verification it is difficult to create confidence. As was so often noted in the context of arms-control negotiations, verification is the most important means of gaining assurance and confidence. Since there is no reason to believe that today's potential adversaries may behave any differently from those of the Cold War, the absence of verification removes an important procedure which could

40

greatly and probably much more rapidly enhance confidence building – which for most advocates is the 'ultimate' purpose of CBMs.

Conclusion: Getting the Most Out of the Least?

There are several justifications for CBMs, but not all agree with the general claims about them. First, it is often suggested that because CBMs are instituted between states that have little or no confidence in one another, they would not be willing (or as willing) to commit to negotiation unless the process was modest and voluntary. While this can certainly be true in a number of situations, it does not apply to all cases. The degree of mistrust or hostility between potential CBM partners varies in each case, and is in fact relatively low in many instances.

Second, the value attached to voluntary agreements is essentially based on assumptions. For instance, whether or not the CBM commitments are legally binding, they do not guarantee better implementation, and those states inclined to accept these requirements will most likely treat them as binding anyway. It is also often noted that voluntary agreements are a more valuable indicator of intentions than obligatory measures. Furthermore, as argued early in the European experience, it is widely believed that 'a legal obligation may be more conducive to minimalist interpretation than a political commitment whose credibility depends on the way in which it is adhered to by the states involved [while] ... a system of political commitments may be more conducive to a *process* of expanded practice as a result of challenge and the possible engines of mutual example'.[47]

As the initial record of compliance with the CSCE CBMs demonstrated, the voluntary nature of the agreement did not deter or prevent Soviet violations, nor has a 'minimalist interpretation' been avoided.[48] In addition, the views presented above seem to diminish, if not contradict, the argument that states would not be as amenable to joining CBMs regimes if they were more comprehensive, as it is those same states which are presumed to provide a more forceful or forthcoming record of compliance simply because the measures are not recorded in treaty form. Furthermore, even if the argument that states do not accept more demanding agreements is based on the belief that their motives for adopting such a position stems from fear of commitment or being obliged to do something they may later regret, is this not a good argument for their clear commitment in the first place, to prevent them from dropping out of the regime whenever they wish?

A third argument is that if the obligations or requirements to be negotiated were detailed and comprehensive, it could deter some states from joining the exercise, or become a source of friction which could actually increase tension. While it is true that attempts to iron out details can provoke acrimony, and that even the most detailed and comprehensive agreements can still leave room for debate, avoiding difficult negotiations in the beginning only saves the problems for a later time and, possibly, makes them more significant once implementation actually begins and the issue becomes politically more sensitive.

The notion that verification somehow goes against the spirit of a confidence-building exercise (or, that it should be kept for a second stage of implementation because of the far-reaching nature of the measures involved at that stage, which usually include restrictions or constraints on military activities) raises profound questions about the concept as a whole. Indeed, there seems to be a logical inconsistency in suggesting that in a pre-CBM phase of application, when there is little or no trust between parties and therefore a need for CBMs, the use of verification mechanisms is less important than in a second phase. The later stage would then follow implementation of a first set of measures which, presumably, would have created enough confidence to move forward, and verification becomes more useful, if not necessary. This, on the other hand, exposes another flaw in CBM thinking, assuming a willingness on the part of the players involved to be reassured of their rivals's non-hostile intentions, despite the absence of verification.

Finally, the above also underscores one of the most important assumptions on which the CBM concept rests, namely that there will be another, second or third, stage of application which will allow the parties to fulfil the more prominent objectives ascribed to the approach, whether arms control, disarmament or conflict resolution. Reaching that first stage is not without difficulties; making further progress will be no easier. The next step is to translate the decisions into practice.

III. IMPLEMENTATION AND APPLICATION

There is no guarantee that successfully negotiating CBMs will result in successful implementation. Like the process of negotiation, the process of implementation has many facets and several issues can hinder its realisation. Implementation, on the other hand, is no guarantee of a constructive or fruitful application of CBMs, nor does it ensure automatic achievement of the goals set for the measures. CBMs do not take place in a political vacuum, and as the measures gain prominence in the field of foreign and security policy, so does their potential for misuse.

Challenges to Implementation
Maintaining Interest?
An important assumption is that once negotiated, CBMs will remain high on the agenda of political leaders, The reality is very different. CBMs may be a prominent agenda item at a high-level public meeting but, once agreed upon, they often become a relatively low priority for national leaders and top policy-makers.

Allowing CBMs to be a low political priority can result in complacency about implementation, with the development of a clearly articulated strategy becoming the first casualty. Ensuring that proper structures are established for managing the agreement, that adequate resources and appropriate training are allocated, that the different agencies or departments with application responsibility coordinate their policies, that consultations with the other CBM partners are pursued in a timely and constructive manner, or that other national policies or actions are consistent with the agreement, are only some aspects of such a strategy which, if neglected, can directly curtail the quality of implementation.

Failing to ensure that a coherent and comprehensive programme of action is planned, designed and executed can produce inadequacies or inconsistencies in application. When coupled with some of the weaknesses of standard first-generation CBMs agreements – such as vague formulations or obligations – an undesirable pattern of minimal or partial implementation may develop, or irregular compliance may evolve. This may bring complaints from other participants of unwillingness to share CBM commitments. If uncorrected, such a pattern can alienate other partners and the regime may completely unravel.

Challenges 'by Design'

Even with a high degree of commitment to the process, effective implementation of CBMs can be circumscribed by the nature and scope of the negotiated agreements. As already noted, the standard design of first-generation agreements include a number of features which mitigate against productive implementation, and equally significant, against a positive common evaluation of the undertaking.

The ambiguities inherent in voluntary arrangements allow each participant the authority to decide the extent to which it will implement the decisions set forth in the agreement. The lack of specificity in commitments also allows each party to judge the conduct of the other partners. Since not all the participants will have the same expectations and the same level of implementation, different patterns of application are likely to emerge. What one state does is likely to become the standard it uses to judge the other partners; in instances where one side takes its voluntary commitments more seriously than others, 'gaps' in implementation may be deemed a reluctance to uphold obligations or, worse, as an intentional breach of compliance.

Implementation reviews, consultative committees, joint commissions or similar methods of considering questions of compliance can help resolve disagreements over implementation. Yet most of these mechanisms do not operate on a regular basis. In the interim real or perceived failures to honour commitments may already have caused some of the parties to draw their own negative conclusions about the value of the exercise, if not to have acted upon them already.

These mechanisms, on the other hand, provide no guarantee that a common understanding of the agreement will be achieved. In fact, they can easily sustain (if not expand) the controversies raised by differing interpretations. The experience of the initial CSCE Review Conferences demonstrate that these forums can actually become platforms for disputes, or for redundant reiteration of national positions, with each side defending its own interpretation and justifying its own record of implementation, with little being accomplished in the way of reaching common understanding on the terms of the arrangement, or on its precise operation. Moreover, in some instances, national authorities may not even bother raising implementation problems. This seems to be the case in both India and Pakistan regarding a number of negotiated agreements in the early 1990s. Their view, it appears, is that to raise issues of non-compliance would give 'more satisfaction' to one than to the other.[1]

In addition to these ambiguities, incomplete agreements or imprecise formulations of particular provisions can produce insurmountable difficulties. Agreements that leave significant activities unregulated, or contain omissions or loopholes, can become instantly irrelevant if any party takes advantage of these flaws. Likewise, procedures allowing for exceptions, or 'escape clauses' can completely negate the usefulness of a measure.

In short, a likely result of incomplete and vaguely drafted agreements will be different interpretations and approaches to implementation. These can then be viewed as a failure to observe obligations or, more seriously, as intentional breaches or violations of the agreements. Such judgement, it should be emphasised, will not necessarily have to be 'correct'. Indeed, by not discarding false allegations or confirming proper behaviour, the absence of verification mechanisms common to first-generation agreements (and described before as the third major weakness of standard design of initial CBMs) can only compound the problems facing a positive, common evaluation of the exercise.

Pursuing Other Goals and Non-CBM Motivations

The original aims and objectives of governments entering into CBM agreements will obviously determine their attitude towards implementation. As noted earlier, there are numerous motives for states to join a CBM regime, but not all will be conducive to producing positive outcomes. If the negotiations have been 'forced onto' the parties, following outside pressure, or have been pursued as a means to gain in other areas, the subsequent implementation (if any) is likely to be disappointing, if not simply misleading.

Two instances illustrate the effects of CBMs being 'forced onto' parties. The 1991 agreements on the prevention of air-space violations and the notification of military exercises negotiated between India and Pakistan, were both reportedly carried out at the insistence of the US.[2] The result has been fragmentary implementation with repeated violations of both agreements.[3]

As CBMs gain importance in many regional settings by becoming the *raison d'être* for several formal gatherings by states to discuss cooperative security, the prospect that states will join the negotiations simply not to be left out of a process which may have an impact on their security also increases. This seems to have been an important motive for China joining the ASEAN Regional Forum, and reversing its previous opposition to a multilateral discussion of CBMs. 'Such moves', however, as suggested by a Western observer commenting on Beijing's new exploration of the idea of cooperative security, 'represent a change only in tactics and not yet in values'.[4]

It is noteworthy that comments by Chinese officials and academics regarding increased transparency in military matters (considered one of the most significant CBMs pursued by ARF members, but one long opposed by China), already point to monumental obstacles to implementation of any measure which may be negotiated in this field. As Chinese analysts point out, 'There is no such thing as total transparency for the military – there is only proper transparency'.[5] Also, when referring to the disadvantages of transparency for weak states, the view in Beijing is apparently that 'there must be different degrees of transparency'.[6] More disturbing still is the claim that *some* information *could* be shared in order 'to make others comfortable'.[7] What such views may already point to is possible 'fabricated' or 'truncated' transparency, which would not only go against the very purpose of the exercise, but could actually be the source of apprehension and possible misunderstanding by other partners.

Finally, implementing agreements for gains in other areas, or as compromises or 'bargaining chips' in a negotiation, can also result in deceptive implementation. No matter how much emphasis is placed on the ultimate successes of the CSCE Helsinki measures, the initial European experience still provides the most important example of a situation where non-CBM motives were the primary reasons many states signed on to the measures, and of a subsequent application that went wrong. Indeed, not only did the former Warsaw Pact nations object to every CBM proposal until these measures were made almost irrelevant, they also disputed or opposed all improvements and used the overall CSCE process for propaganda and unilateral gains. They also provided a pattern of implementation which, by making continuous use of its many flaws and weaknesses, only served to reinforce previously held patterns of mistrust.

Challenges 'From Within'
Obstacles to constructive implementation will not be limited to low political priority, porous and sketchy agreements, differing motivations or even to factors related to inter-state implementation. Internal political and bureaucratic considerations will play an important role in this process, and can greatly undermine its effectiveness.

Domestic Politics

A change of leadership certainly ranks high on any list of domestic issues which can challenge the pursuit of a negotiated CBM regime. While all inter-state arrangements are similarly hostage to such changes of circumstances, the voluntary and non-legal nature of most CBM agreements make them particularly vulnerable to any such changes. Indeed, the less formal the nature of the undertaking, the more ambiguous the status of the obligations. The more vaguely drafted the provisions, the easier it may be for new national authorities (or even existing ones) to re-evaluate commitments or re-interpret provisions. CBMs are also not immune to changes in the political climate, or to changes of policy. In this regard, deficiencies in agreements can also allow reconsideration or defection. Finding ways to let commitments 'slip' is much easier (and politically less costly) than their complete and public repudiation, especially if the agreements, like most initial CBMs, are not registered in treaty form.

Outside Reliance

Other difficulties which can arise from domestic considerations may have little to do with politics. Financial, technical or organisational problems are cases in point. These are rarely mentioned in CBM discussions, but they can nevertheless create an inability to undertake, or to sustain, a regime.

An aspect of the Middle East peace process illustrates that CBMs do not always come 'cheap'. In the context of helping to facilitate the development of maritime CBMs in the region, Canada was asked in May 1994 to organise a practical cooperative Search and Rescue (SAR) and INCSEA demonstration.[8] Taking place off the coast of Venice, Italy, in July 1994, the demonstrations involved a Canadian frigate and a US Navy support ship, as well as an Italian maritime patrol aircraft. Although the 15 participating regional delegations had agreed to the demonstrations a few months earlier, only four actually came to observe the simulations. As one participant noted, this was a major disappointment 'to all of those who re-scheduled ship time to make these expensive platforms available'.[9] Fortunately, this 'disappointment' did not diminish the commitment of the extra-regional powers involved to support fully the establishment of CBMs in the region. The episode does emphasise, however, that the practical operation of certain measures and even, as in the case here, of one simple demonstration, is not necessarily 'free'. Many nations, it should be recognised, could probably not even afford the 'luxury' of such simulations. In fact, it is not uncommon to hear representatives of Third World countries say that they could not manage the number and level of obligations entailed in the European OSCE CSBM regime.

If outside support can offer a solution to limited resources, it may not necessarily be available, nor always a blessing. The latter seems to be the case of the Regional Security System (RSS), a collective security endeavour established by several East Caribbean nations in 1982.[10] As agreed from its inception, the primary aim of the RSS is 'to prepare contingency plans and assist one another on request in national emergencies ... [or in cases of] threats to national security', as well as a host of other situations, including search and rescue, protecting off-shore installations and preventing smuggling.[11] Since 1985, the RSS member states, along with other Caribbean nations, the US and other countries at various times, have held yearly military training exercises. These exercises, however, are not planned or devised by the RSS countries, but by the US. 'Because of this, RSS (and Caribbean) interests are not central but peripheral to their overall goals'.[12] Furthermore, given the limited resources of the RSS member-states, heavy reliance on foreign assistance is necessary. While such support has been granted in the past by a number of countries, including the US, the UK and Canada, a reduction in contribution by the latter two is said to further jeopardise this body.[13] The result of all of the above is that 'although reduced, the nature and level of foreign support not only compromise the interests of the System, but also its operational readiness, and consequently its ability to fulfil its multidimensional mandate'.[14]

Executing Implementation
Daily operation will be the ultimate challenge to implementing successfully CBMs. There are numerous ways in which any particular CBM can go wrong, but four interrelated general aspects are worth mentioning.

First, as already discussed, many CBM agreements do not contain clearly defined procedures for practical operations and often only suggest vague 'obligations'. An agreement simply calling for the 'voluntary' exchange of observers at military manoeuvres may, or may not, result in such observation taking place. Moreover, the same provision, without further details or concrete instructions on how it should actually take place, may allow for a wide variety of practices. Who should be invited, what they should be allowed to see, how, and for how long are only a few of the many practicalities which will determine whether such an effort is worthwhile.

A second issue is that difficulties ensuing from sketchy agreements can be directly passed on 'to the ground'. Indeed, unless national authorities provide comprehensive instructions which go beyond what have been agreed with the CBM partner, these problems will have to be dealt with 'in the field', where great latitude for interpretation may be left to many different levels of bureaucracy or, at times, to the lowest level of political power.

Finally, CBMs cannot always be pre-formulated with clear instructions for use, nor are they always able to be directly, constantly and instantly monitored by the highest levels of political power. INCSEA agreements, for example, though functioning on the basis of pre-agreed codes, can only be subject to the strictest political control if aggressive surveillance, which accounts for the great majority of incidents at sea, is forbidden by the national authorities concerned. If such operations are not completely abandoned, the ultimate responsibility for implementation lies directly with the naval commanders involved. In the case of the US–Soviet INCSEA agreement, activities which had previously caused such incidents were not abandoned altogether, with the result that the number of serious incidents continued to be fairly high, about 40 in 1983, compared with over 100 annually in the 1960s.[15] Many of the 1960s incidents were reported to have been created by 'the excessive zeal or incompetence of naval officers'.[16] While this clearly underlines the importance for national authorities to ensure that adequate training is provided, it also reveals that even with such training serious incidents *will* continue to happen. What is more important, however, is that the danger in the recurrence of such incidents is not simply that of a possible failed CBM, but the possibility that in a time of crisis 'commanders ... can be expected to watch closely for violations of CBMs [and that] local commanders could then use any violations, perceived or real, to justify "compensatory" or escalatory actions they take on their initiative'.[17] This would have a possible net result of making worse (if not of provoking) the kind of situations the agreement was meant to avoid in the first place.

Other examples of CBMs which are even less amenable to any pre-agreed, clear instructions or to constant and instant direct political oversight, are hot-line systems established between military headquarters, sections of the armed forces, or for use by local commanders.

One account of such use reveals disturbing aspects about the practical use of some CBMs and the risks inherent in the great latitude of operation of certain measures. Following a skirmish in the disputed area of the Siachen glacier, India reportedly used the hot line to notify Pakistan that approximately 40 of its combatants had died. Initially denying that any military involvement had taken place in the area, Pakistan made use of the hot line the following day to inform India that a military mission would be arriving to retrieve the dead. Probably in reaction to the initial communication, India replied that it had no knowledge of any fatality, or that any incident had taken place in the area. This unfortunate and gross misuse of a dedicated communication link, while not escalating the situation, nevertheless underscores such a possibility. It also stresses the risks inherent in the latitude of operation of certain CBMs.

Challenging Outcomes
The successful application of CBMs does not come with the signing of an agreement. In fact, while even the most forthcoming and forceful implementation can create problems, anything less can call the regime into question. Indeed, unless all parties are ready to sustain differing, minimal or partial implementation, or irregular compliance, the outcome of the exercise may be much more serious than simply and quietly discontinuing the process. Fragmented implementation may result not only in accusations of unwillingness to share commitments, but it can also be interpreted as a violation of the agreement which, if acted upon, can have grave repercussions.

In this latter regard, the potential negative consequences of confidence-building measures are not limited to the above considerations where the effectiveness of a regime can be challenged by what may be described as predominantly involuntary actions. CBMs can also be challenged by an unwillingness of one party to an agreement to participate fully in the process or, alternatively, to use it to gain key advantages against its CBMs partner.

Improper and Negative Use of CBMs
When reviewing the application of CBMs, the possibility remains that such systems may be used for purposes other than simply creating confidence. In this manner, adopting a CBMs regime can have an adverse impact on confidence and security. The most potentially dangerous effects relate to military risks.

Military Risks

There are at least three ways in which a CBM regime can work against the security and military goals set for them: selective compliance, bad faith and deception. The potential risks and drawbacks incurred by such negative compliance are predominantly associated with implementing initial measures. These would most likely be carried out with less than comprehensive verification (if any at all) and would also, as a general rule, be voluntary or non-binding commitments.

Selective Compliance

Like minimal, partial and irregular implementation, selective compliance may be based on omissions in agreements, vague formulations, exception clauses or loopholes which allow parties to interpret or apply the agreement with great latitude. Unlike the difficulties noted before which would evolve largely as a result of inadvertent actions, selective compliance implies intentional use of these weaknesses or loopholes. The 1991 Agreement between Pakistan and India on the Prevention of Air Space Violations provides an example of permissive language which can be used to justify selective compliance.

Article 1 of the Agreement stipulates that 'both sides will take adequate measures to ensure that air violations of each other's airspace do not take place'.[18] Immediately following this opening sentence, however, (and directly diminishing its impact), the agreement notes the possibility of 'inadvertent violation'. While such an 'escape clause' may be necessary to avoid over-reaction to the odd case of a trained military air force officer flying off-course during a routine mission, the provision nevertheless opens the door to justify continued violations.

According to a senior Indian official, the number of air-space violations has decreased significantly since the agreement was signed. From approximately 100 violations per year, there were only some 20 by 1995. While highly commendable, it should be recognised that air-space *violations* do not necessarily happen *inadvertently*. Like 'incidents' at sea, these violations often follow from a well-established military practice in which air-space transgressions can be useful – and are used – to test the readiness of the other's air-defence system. As commonly recognised, such flights can 'yield valuable operational intelligence about system reaction times, radar locations and frequencies'.[19] In the case of the India-Pakistan agreement, violations may also occur as each side 'monitors' activities in disputed areas.

Taking all of the above into account, what the 20 or so violations per year seems to suggest is a clear intent to continue such practices; the implications are significant. If viewed only in probability terms, the fact that the number of air-space violations has been reduced five-fold in a few years certainly decreases the number of potentially dangerous incidents which may result from such transgressions. What it does *not* do, however, is remove these dangers. Furthermore, from a strictly military point of view, if the purpose of such an agreement is to reduce the risk of 'inadvertent' intrusions being interpreted as preparation for attack resulting in escalatory actions, the continuing number of violations does not make the situation any less de-stabilising, nor any less threatening.

From a political point of view, what such a selective pattern of compliance will *not* do is build confidence in the viability of the agreement or, for that matter, build confidence in the trustworthiness of the other side to adhere faithfully to any other agreement which may have been negotiated between the two nations. In the case of the Indo-Pakistan agreement, the arrangement supersedes 'all previous understandings in so far as air space violations ... are concerned'. A partially implemented agreement meant to replace another partially or non-implemented agreement can only create more mistrust and suspicions between rival states.

Another example of selective compliance with a CBM agreement is how a hot line is, or is not, used. While no pre-formulated or pre-agreed scenarios can be devised for using such systems, and the decision as to when a situation warrants such use is highly circumstantial and left to the discretion of the parties involved, refusal to respond to a communication can be especially dangerous. Not only may such action convey the wrong signal, but it could do so at a time of crisis, when the possibility for miscalculation is likely to increase. Yet at least one such instance has been reported, when the Chinese refused 'in March 1969 to accept Soviet prime minister Kosygin's "hotline" call following Sino-Soviet border clashes'.[20]

Bad Faith

A selective pattern of compliance, although undesirable and potentially dangerous, cannot be regarded as a violation of an agreement. Bad faith, on the other hand, although not entailing any clear violation of any provision, is a more serious transgression of generally accepted principles. The difference between bad faith and selective compliance is that bad faith occurs when a state technically complies with an optional CBM, but in fact subverts the intent of the discretionary provisions. Past uses of a hot-line system between India and Pakistan illustrate this. It has been reported, for instance, that on several occasions at time of great tension between the two countries, 'important information was not being communicated over the hotline in a timely fashion',[21] or was intentionally not communicated at all.[22] Presumably, to avoid repetition of this, both countries agreed in 1991 that the hot line linking their Directors General of Military Operations (DGMOs) would be used on a weekly basis to exchange information on a wide range of military issues, including military exercises, manoeuvres, cross-border firing or intrusions and air-space violations. Yet, by mid-1996, the DGMOs were reportedly using the system only to communicate insignificant information,[23] despite continuous and regular reports of mortar fire across the Line of Control in Kashmir, and accounts of several helicopters in the Siachen area being shot down.

Deception
The much more serious possibility of deception whereby a state would use CBMs to provide false indications of peaceful intent cannot be ignored. As part of an Agreement between India and Pakistan on the Prohibition of Attack against Nuclear Installations and Facilities, both sides agreed to notify the other of the latitude and longitude of their nuclear installations and facilities. When information was exchanged for the first time in 1992, 'each side reportedly left off one enrichment facility'.[24] Given the fact that 'a fairly accurate list of nuclear installations in India and Pakistan had been in the public domain for some time', it is unclear whether this should be viewed as a premeditated and deliberate attempt to deceive.[25] Yet what such behaviour clearly demonstrates is a propensity to commit gross and flagrant violations, even of the most straightforward agreement.

What selective compliance, bad faith or the general practice of deception may trigger is, of course, unknown. What is certain however, is that the more important the issue at hand may be for a state and its national security, the more serious its reaction may be. In this regard, the military risks inherent in applying CBMs are not confined to intentional misuse of measures. Without verification, any suspicion of non-compliance, or unintentional breach or violation, can also trigger undesirable reactions. More disturbing yet, even with full compliance, many CBMs still leave room for misinterpretation. For example, the outcome of a hot-line exercise carried out to familiarise Middle East peace process participants with dedicated communication links resulted in a declaration of war.

Political Misuse

In addition to adverse effects on security, CBMs may also have negative consequences in the political sphere. As they assume more significance in political dealings between nations, the possibility that they can be used to advance other political purposes also increases.

Bargaining Chips and Linkage

Although their currency may not yet be of the greatest value, CBMs can be used as 'bargaining chips' to achieve gains in other areas.

In 1989–90, the Soviet Union made several overtures to Japan to negotiate a number of CBMs. These overtures were 'summarily declined' by the Japanese, reportedly for 'the same reason that they have consistently refused to establish normal bilateral relations with the Soviets, namely, their claim to the Soviet-held Kurile Islands'.[26] As one analyst observed, 'The Japanese appear intent on using the prospect of negotiating CSBMs with the Soviet Union for the opposite purpose for which they are normally intended, that is, as a bargaining chip to secure a political goal rather than a means to lower tension as a prelude to political accommodation'.[27]

In 1996, in reaction to the US holding to its position not to transfer 28 F-16 fighter aircraft to Pakistan because of reported nuclear non-proliferation violations, former Pakistani Prime Minister Nawaz Sharif stated, 'A rush judgment on this matter could set back all the confidence-building measures that the Pakistani government has undertaken in the past several years'.[28] While clearly a reference to the fact that the US may have been more than just 'instrumental' in the CBM negotiations on the sub-continent, Sharif's comments (along with the Japanese example) underscore what could become a common use of CBMs in the future, namely as a useful bargaining tool – even if used only when everything else has failed.

Similarly, as CBMs gain importance in the relations between states, the threat of discontinuing, or postponing, implementation can become a more common mode of 'retaliation' to protest, or to condemn the actions of other partners in a number of fields.

Deflection and Propaganda

That CBMs can be exploited to deflect discussion on more significant security issues is another alarming misuse of the process which cannot be dismissed. China's 'new found' motivation for entering into multilateral CBMs discussions in Asia is believed by some to be a tactic to postpone, or to preclude, discussion of measures which could affect Beijing's military might.[29]

Likewise, given the ease of most CBM projects, joining an enterprise which may require little effort can also become more widely recognised as an easy way to justify not doing more. In view of their potential for asymmetrical impact, CBMs can also easily be used as propaganda tools to require more of some parties and less of others.

Whereas there are a number of ways in which CBMs can be manipulated for other political purposes, or for immediate gains, there are several more profound and lasting ramifications ensuing from current application.

Unexpected and Unintended Outcomes
Justifying Dangerous Activities
In a peculiar way, a significant effect of many CBM applications is the legitimisation of the military activities they were meant to 'control' in the first place. Indeed, because the primary purpose of most first-generation CBMs is simply to increase transparency about military activities, while their constraints or prohibitions are reserved for later stages of application, the immediate or short-term effect is to justify pursuing military activities which were formerly considered dangerous. One Western observer commenting on the notification of large military exercises in Europe rightly pointed out, 'Simply knowing from the Soviets in advance that they are conducting manoeuvres is no guarantee that confidence will be built. If a suspected adversary tells you he has a gun, even shows it to you, that does not necessarily lessen your apprehension, much less your mistrust of his motives for brandishing the weapon'.[30]

Exonerating the Arms Race
Another perverse way in which CBMs can work against their intended purposes or long-term objectives is in exonerating the development of an arms race. This seems to be the case with the ASEAN member-states for whom transparency in military matters is increasingly being perceived (and depicted) as a sort of infallible remedy, or 'antidote', for preventing a spiralling arms race. Indeed (and in a somewhat twisted and simplistic manner), it is repeatedly suggested that the ASEAN nations' ever-growing acquisition of new and sophisticated weapon systems should not cause concern because they have embarked on the road to military transparency.

Yet, if there is any validity in the belief that an open arms race is different, or less dangerous, than a secret one, the type of transparency currently offered by the ASEAN nations is not very convincing. When, as was suggested in discussions with officials from some of these nations, the acquisition of an aircraft carrier is justified as a platform to carry out search- and-rescue missions in the region, scepticism has to prevail. What kind of assurance can this form of contrived transparency offer to neighbouring states, especially when relations between many contain unresolved issues and a fairly healthy load of suspicion and apprehension? Unlike capabilities, intentions are not readily verifiable, and intentions can change more quickly than attempts to control the arms races can produce results.

Codifying CBMs: A Stamp of Approval to Do What?
The unpleasant 'surprises' of CBMs may still come in different forms. One, which may soon become be more obvious, stems from the practice of indiscriminately codifying as 'confidence-building measures' a large number of activities designed to bring closer collaboration between states. Exchanges of military missions or personnel, for instance, are widely hailed by advocates as important measures for improving confidence between states. Yet, in many cases, these exchanges have a much more specific purpose and, perhaps, a different objective. The adoption of a plethora of CBMs between China and Russia has been regarded by advocates as important contributions to the recent warming of relations between the two neighbours. In 1994, for instance, there were several exchanges of military missions and delegations, reportedly on a monthly basis.[31] The fact that during some of these so-called 'confidence-building exchanges' visiting Chinese military delegations examined and expressed interest in purchasing a wide variety of military systems, including an aircraft carrier and submarines, may not, however, be reassuring for all, nor for long.[32] Similarly, the fact that 'Russian engineers have returned to upgrade defense factories constructed during the 1950s, and to help modernize several Chinese weapons systems',[33] while certainly making great confidence-building for Sino-Russian relations, will not result in increased confidence for other nations in the immediate area and beyond.

Finding New Partners or Creating New Uncertainties?
As implied above, CBMs may not be seen in the same light by all states, most especially by non-participants. Certainly, the profusion of CBMs

negotiated between India and China does not give Islamabad much confidence,[34] especially since India is also said to be taking advantage of the process to raise the issue of Chinese sales of advanced weapons to Pakistan.[35]

Likewise, in 1991, Singapore objected strongly to a 12-day Malaysian–Indonesian military exercise in Johor, just 20 kilometres from Singapore. It accused Kuala Lumpur of 'insensitivity for holding such major manoeuvres close to the republic'.[36] Some CBM enthusiasts contend that the perceived 'insensitivity' was due to the exercise being carried out without prior notification.[37] However, Singapore may have regarded the same 'pre-notified' exercise as nothing less than a premeditated, organised and provocative military demonstration. As CBMs help create new partnerships, other states may be left out of the process.

Postponing and Precluding Alternatives
Undoubtedly, the most important long-term issue raised by the application of CBMs relates to their wide, positive appeal and the possibility that the approach began to be emphasised to the detriment of other diplomatic or security initiatives. There is already a widespread belief that CBMs are the first step in improving relations between states, implying indirectly that they should be used before other attempts are made to resolve a security issue. Increasingly, many suggest that if CBMs cannot be implemented or bring about any positive results, nothing else will, implicitly suggesting that nothing else should be attempted. The danger with these views is that CBMs may be chosen to the detriment of other policies or measures, not only deferring their application, but also perhaps excluding them.

In this regard, it has certainly become fashionable since the end of the Cold War to suggest that confidence-building measures should be applied *before* arms-control and disarmament efforts. Yet, there is no serious basis for the belief that CBMs can lead to arms control agreements. Several negotiated arms-control agreements were in existence long before any formal confidence-building arrangements came to light.

Arguably, of course, there has always been some form of confidence-building measures between nations, long before they were labelled as such. This point is worth emphasising because the objectives and techniques of confidence-building measures are not new or unique. Reducing the risk of war, exchanging information or agreeing on rules of behaviour are not within the privileged domain of CBMs. They have long been important goals or instruments of many inter-state arrangements or endeavours. As such, if having CBMs *before* arms control, disarmament or conflict resolution (another long-term goal of many CBMs) is meant to improve some inter-state relations before states can begin to limit weapons, disarm or resolve conflicts, and if CBMs are the means to this end, then it becomes imperative to take a closer look at how, precisely, they are being used and what is being achieved. There are many ways they can go wrong, and if they do, they may only end up assisting or postponing rather than promoting the achievement of the most prominent goals ascribed to the undertaking.

The Worst of Both Worlds?

Negotiated agreements are only the beginning of a long process towards the successful use of CBMs. Negotiated agreements are worthless if not implemented, and potentially dangerous if badly implemented. Too often neglected while promoting process over outcome, implementation remains crucial for the fruitful and productive employment of CBMs. It is only by fulfilling the mutually agreed commitments and obligations that states can demonstrate their peaceful intentions, remove threat perceptions, decrease the possibility of misunderstanding and build confidence. While numerous issues can detract from effective implementation, even assuming scenarios of minimal interference, successfully employing CBMs is far from guaranteed.

Initial agreements are often minimal, with limited obligations, loose formulations, no constraints and no verification. Given such features, it is difficult to anticipate that the implementation of CBM agreements will be straightforward and reassuring for all parties, as this requires nothing less than a willingness on all sides to be reassured of the intentions of their rivals.

Furthermore, while the effectiveness of confidence-building measures may depend upon strict and air tight agreements, as well as on the most forthcoming and cooperative compliance behaviour, any variation in these conditions can work against the goals set for the measures, and can create problems. Faulty implementation between partners who do not trust one another can only produce new grounds for charges and counter-charges of non-commitment or non-compliance. In this respect, unsatisfactory implementation of CBMs can quickly consume any confidence while creating possibilities for more, rather than less, misunderstanding.

If the above considerations raise serious questions about the proficiency of many CBM experiments to reach a second stage of application and bring states closer to achieving the higher goals, including arms control and conflict resolution, then CBM applications also have accompanying ramifications. The potential improper uses of CBMs are numerous and even the most 'innocent' measure can become a valuable, manipulative tool to different ends. CBMs can also justify a state taking no action on core issues. Here, perhaps, lies the most important drawback of an uncritical search for CBMs, especially if the possible result would be to postpone the much more pressing consideration of the root causes of the security problem the undertaking was meant to address.

CONCLUSION

Confidence-building measures are worth pursuing, but there are many ways in which they may be ineffective, or even counterproductive. Most examinations do not even consider that CBMs can have an ambivalent or even negative result. For the true believers, they do not fail; they just take time.

The problems with confidence-building measures begin with their convoluted history, which has been characterised by an endless accumulation of promises. What started in Europe during the Cold War as simple measures to deal with specific security concerns became, after the East–West conflict ended, strongly promoted instruments for changing perception and improving inter-state relations. This qualitative leap in the supposed proficiency of simple measures is difficult to explain. Whether the important changes in the international security environment justified these extra aspirations is far from certain. What is clear, however, is that a major and unfortunate outcome of this compilation of promises is that the precise goals – and how they should be implemented – have been lost. While most CBMs are still recommended primarily for use in the military field, it is often unclear whether the measures are seen, and used, primarily as security-enhancing mechanisms, or as tools to enhance cooperation and work towards better inter-state relations. Yet using CBMs to promote cooperation or dialogue between states does not necessarily improve security. This does not mean that existing practices cannot bring positive results for both. The Europe of 1996 provides clear evidence that CBMs can, in some particular circumstances, make a useful contribution to security and help improve cooperation. That CBMs can bring benefits is undeniable. Just because they rarely meet their most important goals, cannot fulfil all of the accumulated objectives set for them, or may often be more harmful than helpful are not necessarily reasons to discard them. However, even supporters of CBMs need to recognise the limits of the concept.

There is a strong sense among CBMs enthusiasts that employment inevitably brings about something positive, and builds confidence. Hence, immediate or concrete results are not as important as the potential long-term benefits derived from starting a process. While beginning a discussion and/or negotiation with rival states or potential adversaries can have important merits, relying solely on the process is a mistake.

CBMs can provide a useful framework for initiating and promoting dialogue between states, while also offering specific opportunities to tackle issues of mutual concern. Yet if CBMs are to address specific issues, sooner or later the discussion has to lead to negotiated agreements. It is one thing to suggest that the process is larger than its sum, but it is a cause of concern when the process is the total of its sum. In fact, a strong case can be made that if a first or newly negotiated agreement is not properly put into practice, the result may be to destroy whatever 'confidence' has been built during negotiations.

Emphasis on the process is not only misleading, it can also be dangerous. Sensible confidence-building measures require that specific action-oriented agreements be negotiated. Agreements need to do what they are supposed to do. If the goals set are too unrealistic, lack of progress can result in disappointment and halt the process. If the agreement is vaguely drafted, it can lead to different interpretations and implementations of its provisions. If flaws and weaknesses are exposed, it can negate the potential usefulness of the measure and call into question the intentions of states. The notification of large military manoeuvres, for instance, becomes useless if any of the parties calls such activities 'movements' and do not declare them because an agreement may not cover such activities.

Agreement on the prior notification of military activities can increase security and promote better relations between states. Such measures, however, are only of use to the extent that compliance with the CBMs provides a benchmark against which behaviour can be assessed. Without verification (which most initial CBMs lack), such a task is difficult to accomplish. It requires nothing less than a willingness on the part of rival states to believe the self-proclaimed, peaceful intentions of rivals – something that CBMs are, in fact, supposed to prove.

CBMs are often presented as if the full potential of the measures can be realised, even though they may be reached only with more ambitious and comprehensive agreements. Initial or first-generation measures, while usually lacking verification, are predominantly voluntary and non-binding. Successful CBMs require implementation to be straightforward and reassuring for all parties. Only the most cooperative behaviour can achieve such results. Anything less than forthcoming and comprehensive implementation can create problems.

Central to most CBMs is the requirement that states exchange information. Communication about military matters is supposed to help clarify and demonstrate peaceful intent, which, in turn, reduces mutual suspicions, increases trust and builds confidence. There is, however, no evidence that such a positive relationship exists between information and confidence; in fact, frequently the opposite happens. Data not confirming information acquired by other means or suggesting a more serious threat than previously believed would not increase confidence, but is more likely to create mistrust and suspicion. Information provided voluntarily, no matter what its quality or accuracy, may not necessarily be believed. In fact, it may very well only bring more questions, apprehensions, and misgivings about what is not known. Not all forms of transparency will necessarily be useful or build confidence. Half-truths about the real purpose of some weapons acquisition are likely to reinforce patterns of suspicions and mistrust, especially if such semi-transparency is under the cover of an agreement designed to reassure others of peaceful intent.

As confidence-building measures become more prominent, they entail certain political ramifications and security risks. CBMs are predominantly concerned with perception and usually do not deal with the root causes of problems. Selecting a CBM policy implies embracing the *status quo*. Unless such a course of action is clearly identified, it should be recognised that CBMs are unlikely to reduce the source of the security risk. How long can the benefits of CBMs exist without resolution of the core issues of contention?

CBMs may also be used to avoid dealing with the security problem. CBMs are often favoured by parties who do not wish to see changes in the *status quo*, but feel obliged, for internal or external reasons, to appear to be addressing the problem. In the context of the ASEAN Regional Forum, China certainly felt strong pressure to join in the discussions of CBMs for which it had never before demonstrated any support. Beijing may not want to be left out of a process which can affect its security and China may see CBMs as a useful tool to deflect, prevent or postpone discussion on more important security matters.

Perhaps the most important issue raised by CBMs is that the measures begin to be emphasised to the detriment of other diplomatic or security initiatives. CBMs could postpone or replace initiatives which may be more effective in addressing the basic causes of conflicts. CBMs are beginning to be seen not as stepping stones to prominent objectives, but as necessary prerequisites. This is particularly evident in the dialogue between the two Koreas where functioning CBMs are seen as a requirement before there can be any dialogue on arms control. On the Indian sub-continent, some argue that CBMs be instituted before any further serious attempts are made at conflict resolution. Adding an extra step in the pursuit of a more peaceful and secure international environment has serious risks. Yet this strategy is currently gaining acceptance with little consideration given to the fundamental difficulties of achieving numerous meaningful CBMs.

Most CBM proposals are based on a number of assumptions, most notably that former, or potential, belligerents *will* have a mutual interest in becoming involved in a CBM process, that the parties concerned *will* reach consensus on the precise content of a CBM dialogue, that negotiations *will* lead to agreement, that agreement *will* be translated into effective implementation, and that implementation somehow *will* eventually bring about the most prominent goals. This set of 'pre-conditions' is cause for concern. CBMs, by definition, are to be implemented between states that have little or no confidence in one another. Unless there is a strong and mutual (*self-*) interest in a particular CBM, the prospect of seeing many 'successes' in the near future may be more remote than anticipated.

These issues are seldom addressed, but they are now particularly pressing. Governments are increasingly turning to CBMs not only because they are not ambitious undertakings, but also because they are seen as harmless and risk-free. Yet, they are not cost-free nor necessarily easy. From the wide array of potential solutions for managing inter-state security, CBMs often entail as much painstaking negotiation and possibility of failure as any other initiative, but with fewer substantial results.

NOTES

Introduction

[1] Throughout this study, the term CBMs is preferred to the more widely used CSBMs, or confidence- and *security*-building measures. The latter term was introduced during the negotiations of second-generation European CBMs, considered to be more militarily significant. However, in other areas of applications, it is often unclear what this term is actually meant to convey, except, perhaps, that the measures are to be applied in the security/military field. To avoid confusion, no distinction is made here between the two terms (unless specifically noted, or in quotations).

Chapter I

[1] The text of the Helsinki Final Act is reprinted in *Conference on Security and Cooperation in Europe: Final Act* (London: Her Majesty's Stationery Office, August 1975).

[2] NATO had no study completed on CBMs before the formal opening of the CSCE. See Albert Legault and Michel Fortmann, *A Diplomacy of Hope: Canada and Disarmament, 1945–1988* (Montreal: McGill University Press, 1992), p. 482.

[3] See John J. Maresca, *To Helsinki: The Conference on Security and Cooperation in Europe 1973–1975* (Durham, NC: Duke University Press, 1985), p. 168.

[4] See *ibid.* See also Bernd A. Goetze, *Security in Europe: A Crisis of Confidence* (New York: Praeger, 1984), p. 77.

[5] Such views were widely held by Western negotiators. See J. D. Toogood, 'Helsinki 1975: What Was Achieved in the Field of Confidence-Building Measures?', *Canadian Defence Quarterly*, vol. 5, no. 2, Winter 1975, p. 29. For a similar observation almost ten years later, see Goetze, *Security in Europe*, p. 78.

[6] Jonathan Alford, 'The Usefulness and the Limitations of CBMs', in William Epstein and Bernard T. Feld (eds), *New Directions in Disarmament* (New York: Praeger, 1981), p. 135.

[7] This issue was only resolved very late in the formal negotiations. For a detailed account of the disagreements within NATO, and the opposition of France and the United States to any CSCE follow-up review, see Ljubivoje Acimovic, *Problems of Security and Cooperation in Europe* (Alphen Aan Den Rijn: Sijthoff and Noordhoff, 1981), pp. 270–83.

[8] This was a dominant feature of the 1978 French proposal to establish a Conference on Disarmament in Europe. For a discussion of the proposal, and the perceived usefulness of CBMs for facilitating arms control, see Benoît d'Aboville, 'Le projet de Conférence européenne sur le désarmement et l'échéance de Madrid', in Pierre Lellouche (ed.), *La sécurité dans les années 80: Les relations est–ouest et le théâtre européen* (Paris: Institut Français des Relations Internationales [IFRI], 1980), pp. 393–403.

[9] Lawrence Freedman, *Arms Control: Management or Reform*, Chatham House Papers 31 (London: Routledge and Kegan Paul for the Royal Institute of International Affairs, 1986), p. 29.

[10] See Les Aspin, 'A Surprise Attack on NATO – Refocusing the Debate', *NATO Review*, vol. 25, no. 4, August

1977, pp. 6–13; Sam Nunn, 'Mutual and Balanced Force Reductions – A Need to Shift Our Focus', *The Atlantic Community Quarterly*, vol. 16, no. 1, Spring 1978, pp. 18–21.

[11] Christoph Bertram, *The Future of Arms Control: Part II. Arms Control and Technological Change: Elements of a New Approach*, Adelphi Paper 146 (London: International Institute for Strategic Studies, 1978), p. 19.

[12] Strobe Talbott, *Deadly Gambits* (London: Picador, 1985), p. 323.

[13] The phrase was probably first used by Ambassador James E. Goodby, head of the US delegation to the Stockholm Conference on Confidence- and Security-building Measures and Disarmament in Europe. See John Borawski (ed.), *Avoiding War in the Nuclear Age. Confidence-Building Measures for Crisis Stability* (Boulder, CO: Westview Press, 1986).

[14] See Paul K. Davis, *Toward a Conceptual Framework for Operational Arms Control in Europe's Central Region* (Santa Monica, CA: RAND, November 1988).

[15] UN General Assembly Resolution 914 (X), 16 December 1955. The term was rarely used until serious discussions on convening the CSCE began in the early 1970s.

[16] US Chief of Naval Operations Admiral Elmo R. Zumwalt Jr, *On Watch* (New York: Quadrangle, 1976) p. 391, as quoted in Sean M. Lynn-Jones, 'Agreements to Prevent Incidents at Sea and Dangerous Military Activities: Potential Applications in the Asia-Pacific Region', in Andrew Mack (ed.), *A Peaceful Ocean? Maritime Security in the Pacific in the Post-Cold War Era* (Canberra: Australian National University, 1993), p. 45.

[17] See *ibid.* See also Sean M. Lynn-Jones, 'The Incidents at Sea Agreement', in Alexander L. George, Philip J. Farley and Alexander Dallin (eds), *US–Soviet Security Cooperation: Achievements, Failures, Lessons* (Oxford: Oxford University Press, 1988), p. 483.

[18] See Allan S. Krass, *Verification: How Much is Enough?* (London: Taylor and Francis for the Stockholm International Peace Research Institute [SIPRI], 1985), p. 118.

[19] United Nations, *Comprehensive Study on Confidence-building Measures,* Study Series 7 (New York: United Nations, Department of Political and Security Council Affairs, 1982), especially paras 28 and 160.

[20] *Ibid.*

[21] *Ibid.*, especially para. 26.

[22] For a comprehensive examination of the discussions, see Dr Falk Bomsdorf, 'The Confidence-Building Offensive in the United Nations', *Aussen Politik*, vol. 33, no. 4, 1982, pp. 370–90.

[23] For a discussion see *ibid.* See also United Nations, *Comprehensive Study,* para. 21.

[24] United Nations, *Comprehensive Study*, especially paras 135 and 136.

[25] Dr Falk Bomsdorf, 'The Third World, Europe and Confidence-building Measures', in Hugh Hanning (ed.), *Peacekeeping and Confidence-Building Measures in the Third World* (New York: International Peace Academy, Report No. 20, 1985), p. 50.

[26] The notification of *Zapad-81* identified a manoeuvre area comparable in size to three times the territory of Czechoslovakia, or some 150,000 square miles. See Victor-Yves Ghebali, *La diplomatie de la détente: la CSCE, d'Helsinki à Vienne (1973–1989)* (Brussels: Établissements Émile Bruylant, 1989), p. 159. For comments on the exercise from the US

representative to the CSCE, see Leonard R. Sussman (ed.), *Three Years at the East–West Divide. The Words of US Ambassador Max M. Kampelman at the Madrid Conference on Security and Human Rights* (New York: Freedom House, 1983), pp. 53–57.

[27] See US Department of State, Bureau of Public Affairs, *Eleventh Semiannual Report. Implementation of Helsinki Final Act. June 1, 1981–November 30, 1981*, Special Report No. 89, Washington DC, p. 14.

[28] See John Borawski, *From the Atlantic to the Urals: Negotiating Arms Control at the Stockholm Conference* (London: Pergamon-Brassey's, 1988), p. 29.

[29] US Secretary of Defense Caspar Weinberger, as quoted in Carl C. Krehbiel, *Confidence-and Security-Building Measures in Europe. The Stockholm Conference* (New York: Praeger, 1989), p. 38. For a detailed account of these activities from a US perspective, see the interventions of Ambassador Max Kampelman at the CSCE, reprinted in Sussman (ed.), *Three Years at the East–West Divide*, pp. 53–57.

[30] *World Armaments and Disarmament, SIPRI Yearbook 1981* (London: Taylor and Francis for SIPRI, 1981), Appendix 17A, p. 495.

[31] Johan-Jörgen Holst and Karen Alette Melander, 'European Security and Confidence-building Measures', *Survival*, vol. 19, no. 4, July/August 1977, p. 148.

[32] Jonathan Alford, 'Confidence-Building Measures in Europe: The Military Aspects', in Alford (ed.), *The Future of Arms Control. Part III: Confidence-Building Measures,* Adelphi Paper 149 (London: International Institute for Strategic Studies, 1979), p. 8. Writing before the events

in Poland, Alford contended that he did not believe this argument to be very convincing because it had 'always been open to a state to announce the holding of manoeuvres as far in advance as it wished'.

[33] Richard E. Darilek, 'Reducing the Risks of Miscalculation: The Promise of the Helsinki CBMs', in F. Stephen Larrabee and Dietrich Stobbe (eds), *Confidence-Building Measures in Europe* (New York: Institute for East–West Security Studies, 1983), pp. 80–81.

[34] Krehbiel, *Confidence- and Security-Building Measures in Europe*, p. 38. The author is referring to the article by Richard T. Davies, 'The United States and Poland, 1980–82', *Washington Quarterly*, vol. 5, no. 2, Spring 1982, p. 146.

[35] For a discussion of the Warsaw Pact notifications, see Ghebali, *La diplomatie de la détente*, pp. 157–60.

[36] *Ibid.*, p. 158.

[37] Goetze, *Security in Europe*, p. 89.

[38] Graham H. Turbiville Jr, 'Soviet Bloc Maneuvers. Recent Exercise Patterns and Their Implications for European Security', *Military Review*, vol. 63, no. 8, August 1978, p. 26.

[39] Christopher D. Jones, *Soviet Influence in Eastern Europe: Political Autonomy and the Warsaw Pact* (New York: Praeger, 1981), p. 113.

[40] Turbiville Jr, 'Soviet Bloc Maneuvers', p. 28. More disturbing, perhaps, Carl C. Krehbali, a military adviser in the US Department of Defense and a participant in the US delegations to the MBFR and the CSCE (Stockholm) wrote in 1989, that it was 'certainly possible that manoeuvres involving more than twenty-five thousand troops could have been conducted by Warsaw Pact members, but not notified, and that any such violations may well not have

been challenged by the West',
Krehbiel, *Confidence- and Security-Building Measures in Europe*, p. 77.
[41] See Aurel Braun, 'Confidence-Building Measures, Security, and Disarmament', in Robert Spencer (ed.), *Canada and the Conference on Security and Co-operation in Europe* (Toronto: University of Toronto, Centre for International Studies, 1984), p. 212; Ghebali, *La diplomatie de la détente,* p. 160; Jones, *Soviet Influence in Eastern Europe*, p. 113.
[42] For a discussion, see US Colonel Jim E. Hinds, 'The Limits of Confidence', in John Borawski (ed.) *Avoiding War in the Nuclear Age. Confidence-Building Measures for Crisis Stability* (Boulder, CO: Westview Press, 1986), pp. 191–92.
[43] The reasons justifying the addition of the term 'Security' have been widely debated over the years. For the views of a former negotiator, see Ambassador Lynn Hansen, 'CSBMs: The Ugly Duckling Remains a Duck – But a Pretty Good One', in Fred Tanner (ed.), *Arms Control, Confidence-building and Security Cooperation in the Mediterranean, North Africa and the Middle East* (Malta: Mediterranean Academy of Diplomatic Studies, University of Malta, December 1994), p. 53, note 3.
[44] See Coit D. Blacker, 'The MBFR Experience', in George, Farley and Dallin (eds), *US–Soviet Security: Achievements, Failures, Lessons*, p. 126.
[45] A notable exception is the work of James Makintosh. This work has featured a strong conceptual and sometimes critical character over the last 12 years. It has focused increasingly on the importance of understanding the nature of the confidence building process and its capacity to structure the potential for change in transitional security relationships. For the most comprehensive articulation of these views, see *Confidence Building and the Arms Control Process: A Transformation View*. Arms Control and Disarmament Studies, No. 2 (Ottawa: Canadian Department of Foreign Affairs and International Trade, 1996).
[46] Kewk Siew Jin, ' Naval Confidence- and Security-Building Measures: A Singaporean Perspective', in Mack (ed.), *A Peaceful Ocean?*, p. 132.

Chapter II
[1] Barry M. Blechman, 'Efforts to Reduce the Risk of Accidental or Inadvertent War', in George, Farley and Dallin (eds), *US–Soviet Security Cooperation*, p. 479.
[2] *Ibid.*
[3] *Ibid.*
[4] *Ibid.*
[5] The 'Organisation of American States (OAS) Document on Hemispheric Security', is reprinted in Augusto Varas *et al.* (eds), *Confidence-building Measures in Latin America: Central America and the Southern Cone* (Washington DC: Henry L. Stimson Center, February 1995), p. 84.
[6] *Ibid.*
[7] As quoted in Andrew Richter, *Reconsidering Confidence and Security Building Measures: A Critical Analysis* (Toronto: Centre for International and Strategic Studies, York University, May 1994), p. 66.
[8] Andrew Mack, 'Confidence-building in the Asia-Pacific Region: Problems and Prospects', in Mack (ed.), *A Peaceful Ocean?*, p. 18.
[9] *Ibid.*, pp. 18–19.
[10] Andrew Mack, *CSBMs and Military Security,* Working Paper No. 83 (Canberra: Australian National

University, Peace Research Centre, May 1990), p. 9.

[11] Brigadier General Javier J. Salazar Torres, 'The Armed Forces and Confidence-building Measures in Chile: Three Essays', in Varas *et al.* (eds), *Confidence-building Measures in Latin America*, p. 66. See also Jack Child, *'Confidence-building Measures and Their Application in Central America'*, p. 16, in *ibid.*

[12] See Legault and Fortmann, *A Diplomacy of Hope*, p. 496.

[13] For a comprehensive discussion, see Krehbiel, *Confidence- and Security-Building Measures in Europe*, pp. 105–18.

[14] See Borawski, *From the Atlantic to the Urals*, pp. 78–79 and pp. 120–21. See also Ghebali, *La diplomatie de la détente*, pp. 181–82.

[15] Kevin P. Clements, 'Conflict Prevention and the Role of CSBMs in the Asia Pacific Region', in Malcolm Chalmers *et al.* (eds), *Asia Pacific Security and the UN* (Bradford: University of Bradford, 1995), p. 36.

[16] At its inaugural meeting in Bangkok in July 1994, 18 countries were represented: the six ASEAN nations (Brunei, Indonesia, Malaysia, Philippines, Singapore and Thailand), the seven ASEAN Dialogue Partners (Australia, Canada, the European Union, Japan, New Zealand, South Korea and the United States), ASEAN's Consultative Partners (China and Russia) and ASEAN's Observers (Laos, Papua New Guinea and Vietnam).

[17] Pengiran Osman Bin Pengiran Haji Patra, 'The Future Course of the ASEAN Regional Forum: Openness and the Regional Approach to Disarmament', *Disarmament*, vol. 18, no. 2, 1995, p. 155.

[18] *Ibid.*

[19] See Parris H. Chang, 'Forging Security Cooperation in the Asian-Pacific Region: A Taiwan Perspective', *Journal of East Asian Affairs*, Summer/Autumn1995, p. 385.

[20] Pengiran Osman, 'The Future Course of the ASEAN Regional Forum', p. 153.

[21] See Michael Richardson, 'Ignoring US, Southeast Asia To Sign Ban on Nuclear Arms', *International Herald Tribune*, 11 December 1995, pp. 1 and 6.

[22] See the collection of speeches and proposals on the subject in *The Mediterranean and the Middle East after the War in the Gulf: The CSCM*, (Rome: Ministry of Foreign Affairs, March 1991).

[23] Suk Jung Lee and Michael Sheehan, 'Building Confidence and Security on the Korean Peninsula', *Contemporary Security Policy*, vol. 16, no. 3, December 1995, p. 274.

[24] See, for instance, Mack, *CSBMs and Military Security*, pp. 6–8.

[25] A similar example is provided in *ibid.*, pp. 7–8.

[26] See *ibid.* Also, *La diplomatie de la détente*, p. 172.

[27] Malcolm Chalmers and Owen Greene, 'The United Nations Register of Conventional Arms and the Asia-Pacific', in Chalmers *et al.* (eds), *Asia Pacific Security and the UN*, p. 139.

[28] See *ibid.*, p. 136.

[29] Although they focus on arms control, two interesting discussions of problems in negotiations can be found in April Carter, *Success and Failure in Arms Control Negotiations* (Oxford: Oxford University Press for SIPRI, 1989), especially chapters 2 and 10; and Michael J. Sheehan, *Arms Control: Theory and Practice* (Oxford: Basil Blackwell, 1988), especially chapter 6.

[30] For a discussion of the Indian position, see the analysis of Charles

C. Flowerree (US Ambassador to the Conference on Disarmament and participant in the UN Group of Governmental Experts on Confidence-Building Measures, 1980–81), 'CBMs in the UN Setting', in Borawski (ed.), *Avoiding War in the Nuclear Age*, especially pp. 107–8.
[31] See Mack, 'Confidence-building in the Asia-Pacific Region', in Mack (ed.), *A Peaceful Ocean?, p. 9.*
[32] For a discussion of China's reluctance to consider naval arms control, or to accept formal, multilateral or constraining maritime CBMs, see Tai Ming Cheung, 'Emerging Chinese Perspectives on Naval Arms Control and Confidence-building Measures', in Mack (ed.), *A Peaceful Ocean?,* pp. 112–28.
[33] Richter, *Reconsidering Confidence and Security Building Measures*, p. 75, note 36, and pp. 65 and 76.
[34] Sheehan, *Arms Control: Theory and Practice*, p. 118.
[35] That such an objective was pursued by the Soviet Union was, in fact, publicly acknowledged in 1992 by a group of senior Russian advisers and academics. See Pauline Kerr, 'Maritime Security in the 1990s: Achievements and Prospects', in Mack (ed.), *A Peaceful Ocean?,* p. 190.
[36] Marilee Fawn Lawrence, *A Game Worth the Candle: The Confidence-And Security-Building Process in Europe – An Analysis of US and Soviet Negotiating Strategies* (Santa Monica, CA: RAND, June 1986), p. 45.
[37] Goetze, *Security in Europe*, p. 80.
[38] See Krehbiel, *Confidence- and Security-Building Measures in Europe*, p. 117.
[39] This issue has been raised by Pakistan since the first round of high-level talks between the two countries in July 1990. See, 'Indo-Pakistan Talks Make "Little Headway"', BBC Summary of World Broadcasts FE/0821/A3/1, 20 July 1990 (Lexis-Nexis).
[40] After the last round of talks, in January 1994, Pakistan said there would no more meetings until the situation improved in the part of Kashmir controlled by India. See 'Pakistan Asks India to Cut Troop Level in Kashmir', Islamabad, Reuters World Service, 19 February, 1994 (Lexis-Nexis).
[41] See, for example, the Vienna Convention on the Law of International Treaties, 1969, as reprinted in Edmund Jan Osmańczyk, *The Encyclopedia of the United Nations and International Relations* (London: Taylor and Francis, 1990), pp. 999–1004.
[42] See John Borawski, 'Political and Legal Dimensions of Assuring CSBM Compliance', in *Symposium on Verification of Disarmament in Europe* (Stockholm: Swedish National Defence Research Institute, 1985), p. 119.
[43] *Ibid.*, p. 118.
[44] *Ibid.*
[45] Darilek, 'Reducing the Risks of Miscalculation', p. 87.
[46] The text of the Agreement is reprinted in Krepon (ed.), *A Handbook of Confidence-building Measures*, pp. 57–58 (all emphasis added).
[47] Johan-Jörgen Holst, 'Confidence-Building Measures: A Conceptual Framework', *Survival*, vol. 25, no. 1, January/February 1983, pp. 4–5.
[48] See Borawski, 'Political and Legal Dimensions of Assuring CSBM Compliance', pp. 118–19.

Chapter III
[1] See Michael Krepon, 'South Asia: A Time of Trouble, A Time of Need', in Jill R. Junnola and Michael Krepon

(eds), *Regional Confidence Building in 1995: South Asia, the Middle East, and Latin America*, Report No. 20 (Washington DC: Henry L. Stimson Center, December 1995), p. 7.

[2] See *ibid.*

[3] Non-compliance and violations of both agreements are widely recognised to be common practice. For an acknowledgement with discussion, see *ibid.*

[4] Rosemary Foot, 'Chinese–Indian Relations and the Process of Building Confidence: Implications for the Asia-Pacific', *The Pacific Review*, vol. 9, no. 1, 1996, pp. 73–74.

[5] As quoted in Banning Garrett and Bonnie Glaser, 'Multilateral Security in the Asia-Pacific Region and its Impact on Chinese Interests: Views from Beijing', *Contemporary Southeast Asia*, vol. 16, no. 1, June 1994, p. 29.

[6] *Ibid.*

[7] *Ibid.*

[8] For more on the maritime CBMs in the Middle East, see Peter Jones, 'Maritime Confidence-Building Measures in the Middle East', in Jill R. Junnola (ed.), *Maritime Confidence Building in Regions of Tension*, Report No. 21 (Washington, DC: Henry L. Stimson Center, May 1996), pp. 57–73.

[9] Private communication.

[10] The RSS was created in October 1982 by Antigua-Barbuda, Barbados, Dominica, St Lucia, and St Vincent and the Grenadines. St Kitts-Nevis and Grenada respectively joined in February 1984 and January 1985. For details on the RSS, see Ivelaw Lloyd Griffith, *The Quest for Security in the Caribbean* (London: M. E. Sharpe, 1993), pp. 155–74.

[11] Article 2 of the 'Memorandum of Understanding Relating to Security and Military Cooperation'. The Memorandum is reprinted in *ibid.*, pp. 287–93.

[12] Ivelaw L. Griffith, 'Security Collaboration and Confidence Building in the Americas'. Paper presented to the seminar European Union–Rio Group Dialogue on Confidence-building Measures, Punta del Este, Uruguay.

[13] *Ibid.*

[14] *Ibid.*

[15] See Alan J. Vick, 'Building Confidence During Peace and War', *Defense Analysis*, vol. 5, no. 2, 1989, p. 99.

[16] Lynn-Jones, 'Agreements to Prevent Incidents at Sea', p. 45.

[17] Vick, 'Building Confidence During Peace and War', p. 100.

[18] 'Agreement between Pakistan and India on Prevention of Air Space Violations and for Permitting Over Flights and Landings by Military Aircraft' is reprinted in Krepon (ed.), *A Handbook of Confidence-building Measures,* pp. 59–61.

[19] Vick, 'Building Confidence During Peace and War', p. 100.

[20] John Borawski, 'The World of CBMs', in Borawski (ed.), *Avoiding War in the Nuclear Age*, p. 36.

[21] Matthew C. J. Rudolph, 'Confidence-building Measures between Pakistan and India', in Krepon (ed.), *A Handbook of Confidence-building Measures*, p. 53. The periods of tension referred to are 1986–87 (following the *Brasstacks* military exercise) and the spring of 1990 (following similar large military exercises). In both instances, the two countries were reported to have come close to the outbreak of a fourth war.

[22] During the 1986–87 crisis, 'India resisted giving information to the Pakistani side out of fear that the information might somehow be misused to its disadvantage'. Kanti P.

Bajpai, P. R. Chari, Pervaiz Iqbal Cheema, Stephen P. Cohen and Sumit Ganguly, *Brasstacks and Beyond: Perception and Management of Crisis in South Asia* (New Delhi: Manohar, 1995), p. 110.

[23] See statement by Robin L. Raphael, US Assistant Secretary of State for South Asian Affairs, House International Relations Committee, Subcommittee on Asia and the Pacific, December 6, 1995 (Lexis-Nexis).

[24] Rudolph, 'Confidence-building Measures between Pakistan and India', p. 55.

[25] Samina Yasmeen and Aabha Dixit, *Confidence-Building Measures in South Asia*, Occasional Paper 24 (Washington DC: Henry L. Stimson Center, September 1995), p. 9.

[26] Richter, *Reconsidering Confidence and Security Building Measures*, p. 65.

[27] Trevor Findlay, 'Attitudes towards CSBMs in the Asia-Pacific Region', in *Confidence-building Measures in the Asia-Pacific Region*, Disarmament Topical Papers 6 (New York: United Nations, Department for Disarmament Affairs, 1991), pp. 68–69.

[28] As reported in Gus Constantine, 'US Urged to Fulfil F-16 Deal: Pakistan's Sharif Fights Further Delay', *The Washington Times*, 15 February 1996 (Lexis-Nexis).

[29] For a discussion on China's involvement in multilateral institutions François Godement, 'Does China Have an Arms Control Policy?', in David Goodman and Gerry Segal (eds), *China Rising* (London: Routledge, forthcoming 1997), especially pp.18–19.

[30] Darilek, 'Reducing the Risks of Miscalculation', p. 74.

[31] See David Shambaugh, 'Pacific Security in the Pacific Century', *Current History*, December 1994, p. 425.

[32] The report on these visits are from *ibid.*

[33] *Ibid.*

[34] See Rahul Bedi, 'India–China: Closer, But Still Not Friends', New Delhi, Inter Press Service, 8 September 1994 (Lexis-Nexis).

[35] Pakistan has raised this issue in almost every round of high-level talks with China. See, for instance, 'China, India Agree to Greater Military Openness', United Press International, 28 June 1993 (Lexis-Nexis).

[36] See J. N. Mak, 'The ASEAN Naval Build-up: Implications for the Regional Order', *The Pacific Review*, vol. 8, no. 2, 1995, p. 319; 'Malaysian Military Exercise Has Singapore Upset', Kyodo News Service, 14 August 1991 (Lexis-Nexis).

[37] See, for instance, Mak, 'The ASEAN Naval Build-up'.